LOSING YOU, FINDING ME

A JOURNEY FROM BROKENHEARTED TO WILD-HEARTED

BY DR. CHELSEA AZARCON, NMD

YAIRUS PUBLISHING HOUSE | YAIRUS.COM

Sharing words of wisdom is satisfying to your inner being. It encourages you to know that you've changed someone else's life. Proverbs 18:20 TPT

FIRST PRINT EDITION | Losing You, Finding Me © 2022 Dr. Chelsea Azarcon, NMD
1   22
ISBN: 978-1-989456-774

Our YPH standard is to always give our honour and praise to God in capitalizing all references to His Kingdom. We will not give any acknowledgement to satan in our grammatical styles or rules.

This memoir is a true story. To protect the identity of persons in this book, identifying details have been changed.

DEDICATION

*To my family. Walt Whitman says, "We were together.
I forget the rest." Thank you that no matter what we go
through our family always comes back to togetherness.*

*To Ellie, the drama of all I have written about was a
soundtrack of your childhood. Thanks for being my friend
anyway.*

*To those who grieve and those whom we grieve: the
depths of our emotions, whether grief or anger, only
reveal to us how deeply we loved.*

*To all the women who have stayed too long. It is never too
late to find yourself.*

TABLE OF CONTENTS

HOW IT ALL BEGAN

It was gloomy. It was cold. It was grey. The first mornings of January always are. I wore an oversized sweater, the color of the weather, with a messy braid flung behind my shoulder. I sprinted through a mist of rain toward the warmly lit coffee shop a few steps ahead of me. In the true spirit of the new year, I had spent the morning cleaning out the garage, and between trips to Goodwill, was stopping for a cup of something warm. I walked through the swinging glass doors, the little bells that hung from their handles singing as I entered. A quick glance around the bustling shop and I noticed my cousin, seated with a group of friends at a booth in the corner. We lived in a small town; an acquaintance sighting was not unusual. Yet, as I spotted them, something inside me stopped. In the soft yellow halo of the fluorescent lights, I saw a stranger sitting with them. He was everything a naive woman might hope a man to look like: Tall and athletic, handsome (maybe a little too handsome), strong jawline, bronze skin, sleek clothes, and blue eyes that were both inviting and full of mystery.

"Why did my cousin not tell me he had friends in town?", I

thought. I was eighteen and these things mattered then. Suddenly, I felt a little more self-conscious about my old sweater, the dark circles under my eyes, and the flyaways in my hair. Quickly, I snapped myself out of it: *"Oh well. I am never going to see this guy again."* With that thought, I held my chin high and, maybe just a little defiantly, marched to the counter to order my drink. Even so, I managed to steal a second glance at the stranger as I passed by him. *"I'm not his type, anyway,"* I thought. By the next day, he knew he was going to marry me.

Seven years later, I watched him disappear in the rearview mirror of my car as I drove away. He stood alone, in a dimly lit parking garage, like a scene from a bad movie. As I had climbed into the car moments before, I tried to hug him. He leaned back as if dodging a bullet. A few minutes before we entered the parking garage, he had been holding me, gently kissing my neck, intertwining his fingers with mine. Now, he would not let me touch him. "It's over, Chelsea," he said.

What happened in between, is the topic of another book. It is a beautiful story—one full of twists and turns, letting each other go and finding each other again. More accurately, it is the story of many books. Over the years, I filled pages and pages with the incredible signs and hundreds of wondrous synchronicities that led me to believe that he was the man for me. I wrote journal after journal, filled with the tenderest ways he loved me. If I told you the whole story, I know you would believe as wholeheartedly as I did, that we would end up married. You would wonder as devastatingly as I did, how we ended up saying goodbye instead of "I do." But I am not going to tell you that story, or how I came to reconcile the wonder of those signs with the reality that played out, because they are not as important as what happened after. Maybe it is better to leave the interim blank, to allow you to fill it with details of your own love story. It is not my love story that is important but my grief story.

This book is a collection of letters and journal entries I wrote the year following my loss of Kyle, including thoughts and stories about those reflections. My therapist encouraged me to write about the grief process—every time I got stuck in it, I was to write a letter or reflection about whatever had me stuck. I directed many of these thoughts to God, others to myself, a few to Kyle. I talk a lot about hearing God in this book and cannot imagine getting through grief without Him. If you have never heard God speak, or you do not believe He does, you might wonder what this is like. I am certain you have felt it before. It is that inner knowing that transcends all circumstances. The feeling that regardless of whether or not it aligns with what makes sense on paper, you know you have stumbled upon the truth. This infuses my story with a wonder that anyone can appreciate. This is the journey of my stumblings in the year following my heartbreak; of how I ascended the mountain of grief and how it changed my heart. This book is a trail guide of the truths I found, because your grief can become your adventure, too. I hope that, somehow, the cries of my grief are part of the song that calls you back to life.

PART I
NEW ERA

FOUNDATIONS

Kyle and I were to be married in September. He picked the date—Jewish New Year's Day, although neither of us knew that at the time. When September came, I did not have a ring on my finger. Instead of marrying, we broke up.

Not long before this, I had felt a strong impression on my heart to pay attention to the Jewish holidays. I am not Jewish by faith but have always possessed an admiration for the celebratory culture of Jewish tradition. In response to this impression, I saved an online link to the Jewish holiday calendar and glanced at it from time to time.

When Kyle and I first broke up, it was not in the parking garage. Like all good breakups, it was over the phone, then in person, then in the parking garage, then with a text, then over the phone again. We were not very good at breaking up and it took us multiple tries to truly end things. In between the breakups, we held hands, talked for hours, went to church together, went to lunch, and held each other. Somewhere in that time, I received a text from him asking if I knew that the date we had discussed for our wedding was the Jewish holiday of Rosh Hashanah. I didn't even know how to say "Rosh Hashanah," much less when or what it was. Immediately, I pulled up my saved link and began reading about this holiday. Rosh Hashanah is the Jewish New Year celebration. This particular year marked the passage from the Jewish year 5777 to 5778. *How strange.* My relationship with Kyle had been marked by sevens. Through the years that we loved each other, there were many break ups, where we were often silent and did not talk to each other. In the last period of silence before our final attempt to work things out, I prayed that if God wanted us to be together, He would bless our relationship in the seventh year of my knowing Kyle. Shortly after I prayed this, I realized that the seventh year was the upcoming year of 2017. Seven months after I prayed this prayer, Kyle and I began dating again. In another seven months, we stopped dating forever.

When Rosh Hashanah came, I was not married but grieving. On New Year's Day of the year 5778, I woke up in a hotel in Los Angeles. The room I was staying in had large windows that spilled sunlight inside. That morning, I stood quietly in the warmth from those windows and looked out. For the first time that weekend, I noticed the address of the building across the street was 888. As soon as I saw those numbers, a thought burst into my head, *"That's funny—8x3 is 24."* I honestly do not know why I thought that, but as I did, I felt the urge to check the time. Glancing at my phone to do so, I noticed the date was the 24th. Suddenly, I remembered that 8 was the spiritual number of new beginnings and 3 was the spiritual number of completion. The 24th then was the combination of those two things: complete new beginnings. With this thought, I glanced back out the window at the building. Posted high above the address was a sign that read "NEW ERA."

This sounds like an epic way to begin your life alone. But it did not feel epic. It felt like I was lost in a wilderness of grief without a map. I did not know how to work through grief or how to rebuild my life. I felt an overwhelming sense of sadness. These letters and reflections in *Part I* are the bricks that formed the foundations of my new life; the milestones were connection points for a map I would later fill in.

GOLD

a month after we broke up for the final time, I opened it. It was a notebook, thin and shiny. The cork cover was sprinkled with shimmering flecks of gold paint that matched the gold edging the pages. It had been a birthday gift from Kyle, left untouched until one October afternoon, when I opened to the blank pages inside and wrote my first reflection.

October 2017

DESTINY

JUBILEE-noun[1]

a) a special anniversary of an event, especially one celebrating 25 or 50 years of a reign of activity.
b) a celebration of such an anniversary
c) a season of celebration

"Jubilee." A word that captures the essence of a gilded celebration. Not exactly the word I would select

---

1   "Jubilee" *Google.com.* Powered by Oxford Languages. Web. Retrieved 3 October 2017.

to describe my life right now. I feel disoriented, like I am living on the inside of a snow globe that has been shaken up. Yet, what is settling on my heart, like little flakes of snow in the moments after shaking, is this word "Jubilee." Personally, I do not have much experience with jubilee celebrations. I have seen a few of them on television shows consisting of things like parades, balloons, and a generalized happy chaos in celebration of a 25th or 50th anniversary.

As this is my 25th year of life, the idea of Jubilee awakens my curiosity. Growing up in spiritual circles, I remember people talking about another type of Jubilee, celebrated by people who considered themselves to be God's people, at the end of a *seven* year cycle. These were far more than a celebration or party. They were a time when losses were restored and *freedom* was celebrated.

Not only am I in my 25th year of life, but I also find myself at the end of a seven year relationship that went terribly wrong. I find myself at an intersection of both time periods when Jubilees are celebrated and although I am experiencing deep loss, it seems that something in my life is whispering *"freedom"* and *" celebration."*

The volume of the whisper was turned up this week, when my friend Song shared her impressions for the month of October with those on her prayer list. Song listens to God deeply and although she has never personally met many of us on her prayer list, she writes words of encouragement for us, borne of this practice, as if she knows the most intimate details of our lives. Her impressions were inspired by this scripture verse— "But He knows where I am going. And when He tests me, I will come out as pure GOLD."[2] She wrote, "In October, an unexpected series of events will lead you to your destiny. You, as one who has been tested and tried, will come forth like precious jewelry, like gold, pearl, or a precious gem. God is bringing a series of events to your life that will help you reach your destiny: the emerging of your calling, your mission, and your new self." Her vision sounds a lot like freedom.

It is interesting to me that the symbol Song used to represent freedom is gold. Today, as I scratched down the definition of "Jubilee" in this journal, I paid careful attention to the gold on the cover and page bindings. These felt like another whisper of promise as the past few months, my journals have aesthetically corresponded to the season of my life. For example, the past year was characterized by dreams. The dreams of my heart were bold, full of possibility, and an unwavering belief that things in my life were working themselves into something extraordinary. My dreams at night were vivid and rich, imbued with a spiritual quality. I recorded both—the dreams growing in my heart and the dreams filling my head at night, in a little collection of journals I had received as a gift. About halfway

2   Job 23:10, New Living Translation

through filling my second journal, I noticed both of the covers were engraved with words about dreams coming true. Today, as I open a new journal to write about a new "golden" future, what do I see on the cover? Gold.

The idea of gold first appeared to me, not today, but in dreams I had during the last few months of dating Kyle. The first time I dreamt of gold was during a weekend when Kyle and I were trying to sort out some complicated issues. I felt unsure if I should stay with Kyle, but was not finished fighting for the hope that we would work things out. Feeling confused, I drove to a friend's house. We processed some, but mostly eased the tension by simply doing life together. That night, as I laid in her guest room, I asked God what to do. When I fell asleep, I dreamt that heaven was preparing my wedding. Although in my heart I was unsure if I would marry Kyle, heaven was preparing as if the wedding was immediate. In the dream, I wore a gown, not of white but of gold. When I woke, I thought this dream meant everything would work out and I would marry Kyle.

A few days later, while he and I were still on the rocks, a friend shared an article with me. The author wrote that she saw those who loved Jesus faithfully, rising from the ashes of their lives, dressed in gold. This reminded me of the gold gown I wore in my dream and it filled me with hope. At the time, I did not notice that the gold the article referred to was rising from ashes, from broken things.

The weeks filled with tension between Kyle and I crawled on, until one day he demanded a decision— by the end of the next week we would either be engaged or broken up. Which did I want? I had wanted to marry Kyle for a long time. Wedding dates and plans had been discussed but there were a myriad of relational difficulties I felt we needed to work through before getting engaged. My belief in our ability to do that was growing in its seeming impossibility, so I again prayed for guidance. That night, I fell asleep and dreamt an angel told me whatever my hands touched would turn to something like gold. But when the end of the next week came, all I saw was ashes—the disintegration of our relationship.

They say gold is produced with great refinement, as the pure element is separated by high temperatures, from the impure components. In the past season of my life, I thought the gold I saw in my dreams represented a promise for the future: a promise for a purified and lasting relationship with Kyle, as the product of our struggles.

Today I find myself at the beginning of a blank page, in more ways than one, and I question whether the recurrence of gold imagery is anything more than a handful of coincidences. Growing up, I used to visit old California mining sites on school field trips, where my classmates and I experienced the actual process of panning for gold. You would stick your pan into dirt and mud, coming up not with hard and certain nuggets, but little flakes—swirling and twirling so delicately in all the mire, you would miss them if you were not looking carefully. Maybe the recurrent dreams and impressions are more like that— handfuls of little gold flakes waiting to be found. They are glimmers of indestructible promise that my future still holds beauty. All along, these "golden" promises have been weaving their way through my dreams to create my future. They have been running ahead of me, even when the outcome of my relationship with Kyle was still uncertain, ensuring that destiny would be waiting for me no matter what happened.

This week, I listened to one of my favorite speakers teach about the exact Bible story on which I have been meditating. The story is about the nation of Israel entering into a land God had promised them. Living in the land was their destiny. The speaker pointed out that at this pivotal moment, the nation's leader of forty years, with whom they had experienced long standing devotion, leadership, and breakthrough, was dead. To move into their promised destiny, the nation had to leave the cherished dead behind. This reminded me of Kyle and my destiny. He was a long-standing source of love and companionship, and I always dreamt he would come with me to the places of promise that my life is moving toward. He had a chance to advance with me and he chose differently. With his choice, his place in my future died. Kyle cannot walk with me into my destiny because I cannot carry what is dead

16

into what is coming alive. But, I cannot let that keep me from embracing the destiny awaiting *me*.

In this story of Israel, there was a river between the people's campsite and the land of promise. Not everyone crossed that river. Some stayed behind and although they did not enter into the territory of God's promise, they were still blessed. Those people reminded me of Kyle. As I step toward the future, it feels like I am creating a chasm of separation between us, much like it would if we were on opposite sides of the river. Crossing into promise means letting go, trusting that Kyle and I will *both* be blessed, even if I move forward without him.

Earlier this week, I placed my hand on my heart. I looked directly at myself in the mirror and resolved aloud, "I will not let what happened in the past become my story. I will live a life of hope." With that gesture, I made the decision to walk toward the freedom and celebration that Jubilee promises.

I guess in some ways, Kyle started this book. I always knew I would write a book about our love; I just never imagined the story turning out this way. But Kyle gave me that little gold journal with its blank pages, where I first scratched down this hopeful promise for days to come. My first few letters are full of hope. My default response to challenges is to start where I think I should end and work backward through difficult feelings to truly arrive there. I found a grace in these words that carried me through the processes of grief. I needed them to navigate a long stretch of days in which it seemed that hope had disappeared. I needed them to set my course before I could allow my heart to free fall into the chasm of grief, which you will see in the coming letters, I eventually allowed myself to do. They were like the final gulp of air you take before going underwater. With time, the words of hope proved true and as I recorded them faithfully in the little book gifted to me by Kyle, I watched my year of grief transform into a year of celebration. To me, such a catalytic process is a little like the process of elemental gold being created. Astronomers believe gold is made through the collision of two neutron stars. These stars are locked into orbit around each other by the force of gravity, dancing toward an inevitable collision and demise. When the stars collide, they create a cosmic ripple, leaving in its wake, gold. That is what happened to Kyle and I. We danced for years in magnetic attraction, then collided, burned, and burnt out; leaving ripples of grief in the space of my heart. Yet, when the dust settled, there it was: strong, shimmering, costly, beautiful. What looked like dust and felt like ashes, was actually gold.

HARVEST

Kyle and I broke up just before Autumn arrived. By the time I started writing these letters, pumpkins were full force in grocery store displays.

There are two contrasting ways to think about autumn and grief. You can think of autumn as the departure of summer sweetness, as the forecast of cold and drab days ahead. Or you can think about it as a time for cinnamon cookies, porches festooned in nature's confetti, a time of *harvest*.

Grief is something like this too. You can think of it as the end to everything you knew to be beautiful in the world, as your induction to dark and cold days of the heart. Or, you can discover it as something else. You can see the lifeless days as a pause still enough for something transformative to break through. You can see this season of grief as a time when the beauty waiting to be developed in your life shines through all the more brilliantly, because of the darkness contrasting it.

This all sounds rather lovely, but at the beginning, nobody experiences grief this way. I was no exception. Kyle and I were nothing if not summer lovers. It seemed our relationship always followed the pattern of the seasons. We loved each other deeply yet were about as different as two people can be. In summer, this difference meant excitement, growth, and relational fireworks of the most wonderful kind. In winter, it seemed to mean struggle, distance, and taking space while we kept flames for each other burning in our hearts until the next summer. I have happy summer memories of my time with Kyle—of picnicking in wide-open fields, lying under the stars, and playing with him in the glassy blue ocean. Fall, however, was always a time that I particularly dreaded, because fall meant transition. Fall was the shaky time when temperatures and passions began to cool and I wondered if we would make it. Given that Kyle and I broke up in September, the autumn following our breakup was no exception to the feeling of foreboding. Yet, it carried with it a more absolute loss than all the preceding autumns of my knowing Kyle.

There is a poem I used to read every fall when Kyle was so often absent from my life and the melancholy tones of the season matched all too well the melancholy tones of my emotions. It came from a book about a love that ran deep but sad and the story twisted all my feelings into something strangely peaceful. The poem is found near the end of the book when the protagonist is on the edge of losing his lover and the impending heartbreak is palpable. A friend sends him and his lover a poem, which they read together, much like Kyle and I read the book about their love story just weeks before ours fell apart. The poem speaks of a grey October sky and compares it to the uncertainty felt in the moment just before you lose everything most precious to you. After describing that fearful uncertainty, the poem reads— "But, if everything is lost, thanks be to God."[1]

"Thanks be to God." I found a heartbreaking reassurance in those words. They stared the future in the face and confirmed what I was most afraid of: everything was lost. Yet, with that, they paired something incomprehensibly beautiful: thanksgiving. Thanksgiving, not the holiday but the actual act of pausing to express gratitude, is where discovering beauty in grief began for me. Gratitude is what connected the seemingly dissonant sides of autumn and grief. It is how winds of change and falling leaves coexisted with the celebrations of harvest festivals and Thanksgiving. It is how sadness and loss coexisted with beauty and joy. It formed the *transition* between those things.

I first began to uncover this type of gratitude with the arrival of Sukkot, which I came to understand as the Jewish version of the Thanksgiving holiday, with a little twist. Soon, I saw that everywhere, God was revealing to me an intrinsic celebratory beauty of fall. It was an earthy beauty in the sense that everything about it was quietly commanding and called for a connection with natural processes that are equally unseen and powerful.

My first Thanksgiving holiday in this new season was something like that—beautiful in a quiet way. I felt a little uncomfortable in my new life where longing for Kyle still very much existed, though his presence did not. In the

---

1   Julian. "If Everything is Lost, Thanks be to God." Qtd in A Severe Mercy. Harper Collins, 1977, p 163.

21

same breath, I felt a joyful anticipation for the promise of harvest I believed Thanksgiving foreshadowed. Before this my family had always hosted big, loud Thanksgiving dinners full of friends, family, and of course, food. Thanksgiving that year was different. It was just my immediate family and a friend or two. I wore yoga pants and a red sweater and we had conversations around the table after dinner had been cleared. I read poetry and thought about what I was truly grateful for. There was a beauty in the simplicity left when what used to be had been stripped away. After everything had been taken, there was still gratitude, still thanksgiving.

If summer was happiness, fall was joy. If summer was giddy, fall was rich. It was not because my circumstances changed but because gratitude gave me a deeper vision for the change surrounding me.

October 2017

CHANGE OF SEASON

Today marks the beginning of the 7-day Jewish Feast of Booths, or "Sukkot". I did a little reading on this holiday and found out that essentially, it is Jewish Thanksgiving. Sukkot is a celebration of harvest and a time to be thankful for God's provision in the wilderness. Known as a season of rejoicing, it forms a harvest festival of sorts.

Right now, everything in life feels inescapably heavy. The winds of season change feel more biting this year, seeming to already carry winter. I have been dreading the season change since September, when Kyle and I broke up. There was something so emphatic about our breakup occurring just before a season of letting go. It was as if God was whispering through nature, "Let go." I do not want to let go. I have never wanted to let Kyle go, never wanted him to fade from my heart, mind, and emotions. I am afraid of what it will be like, when all traces of him are truly gone.

So, I prayed. I unloaded all my messy confusion and hurt to God and, in return, the phrase "harvest festival" emerged in my heart. I thought about the harvest festivals I attended as a child. There was music and games, costumes and candy. There was *celebration*. It reminded me that fall is a time of release but also a time full of celebration and beauty, with thanksgiving and harvest. How strange it is that those things can exist together. In this impression, I felt like God was telling me this would be a *harvest season* for me: it would be fun and joy-filled.

As an echo of this promise, I received a surprise package in the mail today. It was from my sister, who had jammed a box full of goodies, with all the exciting and happy things of fall. There was a dish towel covered in cheerful pumpkin motifs, cozy Halloween socks, festive candy, a warm shirt, and woodland creature prints. With it, she sent a card that read, "I am *thankful* for you." She wrote that she found no coincidence in the fact that so much change was occurring in my life during the season in which we lose the old and prepare to gain the new, later in spring. When I had finished unwrapping all the gifts stuffed inside, I decided to collect the fall leaf confetti she had sprinkled into the bottom of the box. I gathered it up in little handfuls to put in a glass box I keep on my living room table. As I was gathering it, I noticed that the confetti was *gold*. This captivated me because leaves are the symbol of loss and season change. Having sensed that this will be a "gold" season for me, there was a wonderfully harmonious irony in the fact that the leaves were not only gold, but also beautiful, celebratory confetti. It was like these little leaves were telling me this season of loss really would become a season of celebration.

From Celebration to Harvest, From Harvest to Celebration

I have a friend named Allie. She used to be engaged and now she is not. Our stories hold painful similarities. Right now, even though she lives far away and we can only talk by phone, she is a lifeline for me. Last night, Allie prayed for me that I would see how I was "ripe fruit." Interesting choice of words. The allusion to produce reminded me of the harvest season. In the midst of loss, the thought of a harvest is a bit provocative. Harvest is a season of fruit that has matured and is now ready to be enjoyed. If this is true, it means there is something good that has come from this loss; ready to be enjoyed right now. It means there is something to *celebrate* here.

Maybe the idea of harvest is provocative because I do not feel like there is anything beautiful left to be pulled out of me. How something warm and rich, like spiced cider, could be pulled out of a heart that is all dried up, is beyond me. But maybe that is what Allie meant when she said ripe fruit. Maybe God is pulling a harvest out of me beyond what I can see or feel.

The Sukkot celebration was also about a harvest beyond what could be seen. After a week of feasting and rejoicing, the farmers would head back to their fields and plant more seed. With its reflection on the harvest within possession, this holiday also formed a promise for another harvest yet to come. The seeds planted after Sukkot were watered by early rains, which prepared them for a springtime harvest. There is something so poetic about the new harvest being developed by rain. It connects the seasons and rhythms of life in a beautifully cyclic way. Rain reminds me of grief; of sadness and tears. It rained unexpectedly the morning after Kyle and I broke up. I always thought Kyle was my life's big harvest—the fruit of my life's love, prayers, and hopes. While I am beginning to believe that our relationship yielded a harvest of sorts, I am also beginning to wonder if maybe Kyle was the rain instead of the harvest. The years we spent together, accumulating challenges and mistakes, were years of sowing and planting, that have produced the harvest of my life right now. The sadness and tears that have come with him will water seeds God is gifting me with in this season, for another harvest yet to come. The grief of one season develops the growth for the next. Nothing is wasted. There is always harvest, always beauty.

In Autumn, the change of season is so invisible yet so tangible. You go outside right before it arrives and you just know in your bones the world is about to paint itself in brilliant colors. The same is true of celebration as a promise. There is something profound about celebrating a new harvest before it arrives, as people used to do on Sukkot. Maybe this is God's way of connecting us with the certainty of its arrival. Maybe celebration helps us feel it before we can see it.

With Sukkot, I imagine they felt the promise of coming goodness as they ate their olives, hummus, and dates (or whatever it was they ate back then). I imagine they heard it in music and the laughter of those they loved surrounding them. In Autumn, I feel the promise of coming goodness through gratitude—through thanksgiving. I feel it in shorter days that turn me inward—turning me to introspection and stillness long enough to notice the colors of the world around me, even if they are different than they used to be. I see it falling out of boxes, imbuing itself into conversations and prayers. I can feel the promise of another harvest like I can feel a change in season, deep down in my soul.

While earth and heaven, seasons and celebrations, interact to create this pattern of fruitfulness in my life, I find myself in this season of Thanksgiving, of Sukkot. A season that is a sacred pause to express gratitude for all that I have at this moment and all the goodness my soul can sense is coming. As I surrender to the season, it is different than what I thought "letting go" would look like. It is less forced. It is more effortless. In this moment, a spot where everything is changing and everything is not yet—I celebrate. From harvest to harvest. Sukkot.

After I finished writing this letter, I read some words Song had written for the people on her prayer list. She wrote how the month of October would be a month of spiritual harvest festivals. That night, I fell asleep under the largest, most golden moon I had ever seen. It hung low in the sky bringing gentle light to the darkness around it. When I awoke the next morning, my friend Heather told me this was a special moon. It was a *harvest* moon.

DOORS

When Kyle and I first broke up, I knew a new life had to be built but I did not know where to begin. I did not even know how to feel. I just felt numb. I was halfway through medical school at the time and my university offered appointments with a therapist for only $12. So, I decided to visit the university counselor. Her name was Sarah. She was a tall, thin woman, who wore flowy pants and cozy sweaters, no matter the season. She drew her feet up into her chair when she talked to you, as if navigating your life problems was both the most natural thing in the world and an intricate, intimate puzzle that you were solving together. Sarah sat across from me and told me to feel. I told her I was afraid to feel. I was afraid that if I opened the door of my heart to grief, I would fall into a bottomless pit and never come up. "I won't let that happen," she said. So, I started learning to grieve. Mostly, this looked like spending a lot of time alone—long afternoons spent painting or watching sitcoms. It meant eating alone so I could taste my food, and buying bouquets of flowers the exact color of my mood. What I am trying to say is that grieving meant making space in my life to connect with exactly what

I was feeling in every moment.

In this process, I learned how to discover *today*. Sadness is mostly about yesterday and tomorrow: yesterday, when what you are grieving was alive in its vibrancy, and then tomorrow, when the pain promises to be gone. Grief, however, is about learning to inhabit the moment because when you inhabit a moment, you can remodel it. When you remodel today, you create a new tomorrow.

October 2017

TODAY

Today, I felt a little sad: lonely, tired, and hurt by Kyle, while missing the joy and adventure of experiencing another person inside of relationship. I came home and sat in my big, comfy chair, while I worked. I called my mom and talked through my emotions. I laid on my bed, ate a chocolate popsicle, deleted Kyle from social media accounts, wore my new slipper socks, looked at pictures of cute houses, and watched a very interesting video about childbirth for an obstetrics and gynecology assignment.

It is curious to me how babies are so often born in the middle of the night, how the doors of life are often opened when everyone is sleeping, and no one is watching. This is what tonight felt like. Tonight, I felt God in the silence and solitude of my new, strange, still little life. I felt Him between bites of ice cream, photos of pink cottages, and scenes of medical YouTube videos. There was something about watching babies, watching life be brought into the world that filled my heart with hope for my own future. It aroused my femininity and my sense of excitement for the hand in hand journeys of love, womanhood, and motherhood. At the same time, I felt an acute sense of loss over an aborted future, one that was lost to me when Kyle stepped out of my story. I felt a longing for a new future in which I would generate people and family inside my own body. I also felt longing for an expired future, where it seems some part of my own heart still lives, still belongs.

Last night, as I was falling asleep, I remember thinking the door to love in my life was open. I cringed at how corny that was but somehow, it deeply resonated. In my waking hours, I have been thinking a lot about doors, carrying an impression that God is opening doors and opportunities to lead me to the people He has prepared for me. I am praying the doors will be exciting and unexpected—that they would be doors I could never have opened myself. I remember the words Song wrote a few weeks ago about God using unexpected events to lead us to destiny. She said, "You will walk through some very interesting doors."

Yesterday, I walked through a door into Sarah's office, the university counselor, and I talked with her about how I could cultivate my womanhood apart from Kyle. She said to me, "I see ripe fruit in you." I shared how this reminded me of what Allie had prayed, and Sarah expanded, saying that she also visualized a cornucopia, the emblem of the abundant fall harvest. As I reflected on this conversation, I understood that I do not need to cultivate my womanhood or the essence of me that gives and nurtures life, so much as I need to walk in it. I understand part of being ripe is that through the challenges I have faced relationally the past few years, God has been developing in me the fruits and qualities of a woman: kindness, beauty expressed in how I treat those around me, compassion, life-giving capacity, creativity. I choose to walk in them and offer them to those around me as a mother would. As I do so, I choose to walk in my destiny.

In learning to discover these qualities outside of a relationship, I see the part of me that was lost to Kyle being found again. Deep down, I hope the future I lost to Kyle, the love and motherhood, can still be found. I hope that despite all the ways I have to learn and grow into a relationship with myself, a relationship with another person is still in the plans for my life; maybe it is just around the corner, ready to be picked. Maybe the cultivation of my womanhood is the door. And I hope to God that when I walk through this door, believing I am ready to be picked, I find that love, partnership, motherhood, and family are also part of my destiny.

Yesterday, I had to take my first patient at our medical school clinic, and I did not want to. I found my inner response peculiar, thinking to myself, *"this is your destiny."* At that moment, it felt safer to continue as a perpetual student than to walk through the doors of what I am made to do. I thought about how sometimes we have to walk through doors into destiny, even if everything is not perfect. I believe that applies to relationships as well. Despite all of the things I am learning in my life, despite everything that is shifting and changing, and everything that is not; despite all of the ripe things I am finding and have yet to find, I do not have to be perfect. I will take the steps needed to walk through the open doors of destiny—to walk through doors where there is love.

This morning, I pondered the theme of destiny, remembering one of my friends just started a music tour called *Destiny*. How apropos. Yet, I also thought of my friend's child who was dying, then about other children around the world who were dying, and of Allie and I, who did not know if we would ever have children. As much as the door for love is open in my life, it seemed like in many ways, life was trying to abort destiny. As I reflected on this, my mom, who knew nothing of my ponderings, called to tell me the word abort had been floating on her heart that morning. I shared my thoughts with her, and she responded by reminding me that her and my dad had met in a band called Destiny. In light of all this, there is a verse from the Bible that seems to ring especially true today. It is a promise written to a barren woman, "But I promise you, no weapon meant to hurt you will succeed,... All your *children* will be taught by the Lord and great will be their peace."[1] And so, for all I have today and all I do not have, I have this. I have a promise that life is ripe, and it can be born anywhere, anytime. Life can be born when situations are imperfect, when things die and fall apart. Life can be born in the watches of the night, in

---

1   Isaiah 54:17a The Passion Translation; Isaiah 54:13 New International Version

the places and at the times no one would expect to find it. Since I am a woman, I can birth life into existence. I can birth it with the sheer force of my nurture, my kindness, my bravery, and my undying commitment to the belief that barren seasons are no match for the life growing inside of me.

This morning, I glanced at the time. It was 10:10 am. I took a picture because it was October 10th—10:10 on 10/10. It just so happened at that exact moment, my mother and sister, across the state, had both seen the same time. We had all taken a picture and all simultaneously texted it to each other. My mom explained that ten is the spiritual number of restoration and completeness, bringing blessings that cannot be contained. My mother, who is a farmer, lost ten very expensive plants recently. Today, she received twenty free replacement plants: double restoration. Tonight, as I prepared for bed, I again saw 10:10 and it reminded me of double restoration—a restoration to myself and restoration to the future I hope for, both of which I thought were lost when I lost Kyle. I thank God because this is the time, *today*, not just this season, but right now. Today, in my quiet little room, wearing my cozy socks, is when I begin to discover restoration in doubled portions and the cornucopia of goodness inside my own heart. Today is the door that opens to tomorrow's destiny.

ANGER

ere is the truth about my relationship with Kyle: I loved him so much and it was *complicated*. It was a seven-year relationship, but seven years off and on, with more time off than on. There were things about relationship with him that seemed too good to be true, especially at the beginning, and things about relationship with him that were awful, especially at the end.

It was Sarah who most bluntly labeled the relationship (I will use a gentler term than she did) as toxic, identifying relational dynamics that were "glaring sirens" for a lifetime of unhappiness. Of course, I had always known that there were some unhealthy dynamics in our relationship and, as we got closer and closer to getting engaged, the warning signals had become stronger and stronger. In response to these warning signs, I could always hear Kyle's voice in the back of my head, suggesting that I was closed-minded, saying that no matter how hard I tried or how many people I talked to with my concerns, their advice was irrelevant because it was given by people who thought the same way I did. It was different with Sarah. She did not share my belief system. It is ironic that the people who did share my belief system were the slowest to oppose my relationship with Kyle. They were the ones to supply understanding, explanation, and grace. It was Sarah and other friends from different belief backgrounds who most vehemently opposed the toxic dynamics of our relationship. Sarah's honesty cut through my mess of emotions and helped me discern the difference between cheap grace and true grace. Cheap grace is what I slathered over all the problems in our relationship that I desperately hoped would work themselves out: generous justifications that allowed me to keep my heart and emotions chained to Kyle. True grace is what I experienced when we were no longer together. This is the expensive kind of grace, won in the wrestling match between anger and longing, love and contempt. True grace is how you hold someone, something, acknowledging all its angles in the light of truth. True grace is how you hold someone or something, when you have let it go. This is one of my few letters to Kyle, one I wrote but never sent. It was the first letter Sarah assigned me and one of the first times I allowed myself to fall into the depths of my emotion. This letter is long, messy, and raw. To make it easier for you, my reader, I have divided it into two parts—the going back and unpacking the anger, then the going forward and figuring out what to do with the mess. What I discovered in allowing myself to experience anger, was that it was one of the first times following our breakup that I felt anything beyond grief.

October 2017

Dear Kyle,

I wanted to write to you because I have been feeling hurt—angry even. I have been talking with the university counselor about grief and how it needs to move. This may be true for anger as well. Feeling anger seems so scary, but I am learning that suppressing it is what makes it destructive.

Counseling has created space for this emotion to finally be heard. In our relationship, when I tried to express an opinion, desire, or need that you were in disagreement with, you often swayed me into thinking I was narrow-minded or extreme for feeling the way I did. I do not know exactly when or how it happened, but eventually, I began to believe what you said about me too. I think I felt such a desperate need for your love, I was willing to believe ugly things about myself to secure it. I walked into Sarah's office ready to accept blame, to add it to the burden of shame I was already carrying. What happened instead is that she looked at me with her piercing eyes and listened to my story in her somehow communicative silence, and told me I was not crazy. I was codependent. I was insisting on loving someone who was not able or willing to love me the way I wanted and needed to be loved.

In your absence, I am beginning to see things that happened in our relationship a little differently. I am beginning to see why none of the people closest to me, not even the ones who made excuses for your behavior, thought you treated me with the honor and respect I was worthy of. I am beginning to acknowledge all the ways I would have liked to been given to, desires I ignored in fear of losing you.

I wanted you to align with me in my process of learning to become a doctor. Something happened the weekend before my first medical boards. I set a boundary and I paid for it. It was summer and I had spent the past month driving between San Diego and Los Angeles to visit you. I was taking on the commute since you had just moved to LA; I helped you as you settled into a new apartment and job. My month looked something like this: Drive to Los Angeles to visit you and fight with you when I was supposed to be studying. Drive back down to San Diego for a birthday party. Go back up to Los Angeles to smooth over the fighting. Take a flight to Northern California to visit family. Back down to Southern California a few days later. I spent the week before my board exams in the oven of Riverside, California so I could watch my kid sister compete in Jr. Olympics. For 8 hours a day, I sat in the 106-degree heat, sweating over an open USMLE textbook, trying to jam information into my brain.

When the weekend before my boards came, I asked you to take a turn visiting me. I was too exhausted to make another trip. I planned to brush up on a few last-minute topics while you sat next to me working and we could enjoy each other's company. I would spend the rest of the time nourishing my body and soul. I had found a church conference I wanted to attend. I was excited about it and asked you to come with me. Your answer to all of this: "no." The discussion somehow became about how selfish I was for not driving to see you. You reasoned that in the time I spent attending the church event, I could have instead driven to your house, so I must be making excuses to avoid a visit. You confronted me: How could I ask you to come to my "boring" apartment? I should come work with you so you would be more comfortable. That weekend, you ended up going out of town with my cousin. I called, texted, and emailed you, begging you not to follow through with the breakup you threatened, begging you not to be angry at the time and attention the pursuit of my dreams took away from you. It worked. It bought our relationship a little more time, but looking back I wonder: why did it have to be all my life arranged around all your terms or no relationship?

I allowed it because I craved your approval. I longed for you to tell me I was intelligent and would succeed. You let me play doctor—practicing my physical examinations on you, listening to your heart and lungs, and you enjoyed telling people your girlfriend was going to be a doctor. Behind closed doors, you doubted the therapies that interested me, referring to them with profanities to show how little you thought of them. You also doubted my potential. You told me I would never earn enough salary to pay off my educational loans and my financial dependence on you would entitle you to full decision-making authority in the relationship.

When you moved back to LA, you said it was to propose. The new apartment, the new job; it was all so you could buy that diamond ring we liked so much, and start our lives together. Sometimes I wondered if that was ever true or if you simply hated Las Vegas and desperately wanted to be back in Los Angeles where you grew up. Before your move, we held hands over lunch on an outdoor patio and talked about all the logistical steps it would take for us to begin our lives together. Step one was a job, step two an apartment. I wanted you to look for a job in San Diego, where I would live as I finished the last two years of my doctorate. We would be married in a few months and I wanted to establish our life together in the same city. You had objections—it would hurt your salary and *all* the jobs in San Diego were the wrong type. I consented but thought an apartment in San Diego would be nice. I did not want to add the four hour daily commute to and from Los Angeles to my already grueling schedule. You refused on account of the commute it would pose for you. I suggested an apartment halfway between San Diego and Los Angeles. No further discussion occurred but a few weeks later, you called me with the "great news" you had signed a lease for an apartment in Los Angeles. I congratulated you. Maybe we would just have to live separately for the first few years of our marriage. But this was out of the question for you. The unspoken expectation was clear. I would move, hours away from my school, to live with you. I would commute so you did not have to.

Once you settled into living a few hours away from me, you had a problem with not being able to see me enough. You framed it so romantically— you just wanted to spend all your time with me. Of course, you considered the fact that this was not happening my fault. You complained that I needed to come visit you more. Because the limitations of my schedule would not allow that, I invited you to visit me during the week. Although your 9-5 schedule sounded like heaven to me, you insisted it was much more demanding than mine. You argued traffic was against you and in my favor, although in reality it was the same in both directions. To you, the responsibility was clearly mine. I was given a prescription for a number of days I was required to see you if the relationship was to continue. My class schedule would not allow that. You insisted I change my class schedule. I explained that, in medical school, you are assigned a schedule and you complete what you are assigned. Change schools, you demanded. I gently pointed out that the nearest school offering my specialized program was out of state and I did not see how that would help us. You reminded me that if I could not figure it out, there were plenty of other girls who wanted to date you.

Just once, I would have liked some respect and support for what I was pursuing. I would have settled for compromise. But my dreams were just another thing I was expected to arrange around you. *And I felt inferior.*

I wanted your comfort and support in the struggles with my own health. I spent years of my life in bed, with pain. I was assessed by doctor after doctor who did not know what was wrong, to eventually be diagnosed with chronic illnesses. I wanted you to see the good life I have lived beyond those things. While we were dating, I was treated by a Stanford Rheumatologist; I was elated with his treatment. Before I found him, I felt like I was dying. Now, I feel better than I ever have. Most people with my health conditions are in and out of hospitals, unable to keep a job. I am functioning better than I have in years, nearing the end of medical school, which is a huge physical accomplishment, even for a healthy person. I wanted you to celebrate those little victories with me. But you insisted I was not getting better because I could not eat pizza with you and I was still too tired to watch movies or go to bars with you, past the midnight hour. I was still not, as you said, "normal."

I thought that maybe if you understood what "chronic" illness meant things would be different. Improvement was exciting, not expected. So, after long days of studying, I read through research articles. I compiled the ones explaining the neurology, biochemistry, and pain perception pathways involved in creating chronic illness and worked on synopsizing them in a review. Maybe if the scientific literature told you to, you would accept me in my fragility.

It did not matter. You claimed you knew what was wrong. I am very close to my mother who also struggles with chronic illness, a similarity which has been a much-needed source of support and understanding over the years. Never mind genetics, you proposed my mother was psychologically manipulating me to make me sicker than I am. Though my blood tests argued differently, you said my health problems were in my head. The solution was to do the things and eat the foods that made me worse because if I was not afraid of them, they would not make me sick.

Because I was "not improving," I would not be allowed to see my doctors after we married. Although I wanted to keep seeing my doctors, you disregarded my preference, with the justification that you would be paying for all my medical treatment (something I never requested of you). I asked if I could at least select the new doctors I would see. After all, I was in the medical field. You were not. I had been a patient of UCLA hospital and Mayo Clinic. I had shared the same endocrinologist with multiple celebrities. I knew who the best doctors were. No, you insisted on choosing them. I felt afraid. Ordinary doctors never knew what to do with me. They prescribed medications to manage symptoms and it never worked. I reluctantly, but conditionally, agreed. If I did not feel right about their recommendations, I would not follow them. It was my body, and I would decide what I was going to put into it. You put your foot down to this as well. You would choose the doctors. You would require me to do whatever they told me. Nothing more, nothing less. No matter that it was my body we were talking about. They knew best. You knew best. *And I felt suffocated.*

When the weight of all these red flags became too much for me, I asked you to go to therapy with me. I wanted to stay with you and thought maybe having mutual accountability would help us work things out. We fought the morning of our appointment. I had made some snarky comments that led to you telling me I was closed minded, unkind, and negative. We drove in silence to the appointment because I was fuming. No one else in my life called me those things. We arrived and when I turned off the ignition, you took my face in your hands and kissed me. "No matter what happens in there, I love you," you said. A romantic gesture. It disarmed me. We were going to be okay. Maybe I was the problem. Maybe if I was better at relationship, we would work. I had scheduled this meeting with the intention of discussing my concerns about our relationship and the ways I needed you to support me. What happened instead was that we spent the entire hour talking about your problems with me. I allowed it because I wanted to be humble and gentle, and own my stuff. At the end, I paid for the appointment and we headed to lunch. Over plates of Thai food, you asked me what I thought the counselor's words to you were. I shared one small thing, a weakness we both knew as true. You denied it. Later, you told me you did not want me talking to that counselor about our relationship. Nor did you want me talking to my parents or my mentors. Because I was the only one in the relationship with mentors, I asked you to seek counsel and accountability, things we desperately needed, to show me you were serious about protecting our relationship. You would not. *And I felt isolated.*

I had a few non-negotiables myself and I feel like you never forgave me for that. Some were misguided and some I still stand by. All were from my heart, from a desire to have the healthiest relationship possible. I wanted you to see the things I asked you for as ways I opened my heart to you; things I was asking you to protect, not a list of demands or ways I was trying to "control" you.

I think of this in contrast to all you asked of me over the course of our relationship. It felt like your love was divided into categories, endless possibilities for ways in which I could fail to meet your expectations. I felt like you were never happy with just me, unable to find joy in aspects of our relationship, beyond the category which made you feel most loved. In that "love language," no amount of escalation was ever enough for you either. So you let me know what your expectations were. After we married, you wanted sex at least 12 times a week. I loved you so I said that might be fun and we could certainly try, but it seemed like an unrealistic goal for every week of our entire marriage. We both had jobs and all that sex would certainly makes some babies we would have to raise, and we might have other interests. If we wanted to be serious about that goal, I suggested we may have to schedule it. That was too unromantic for you. You wanted all of it to be spontaneous. I entertained the conversation because I wanted you to know I desired you. But, deep down, I did not want anyone telling me how many times I would have to sleep with them. *And I felt uneasy.*

There are so many ways in which I felt alone and isolated in our relationship. I felt alone in my career pursuit, alone in my pursuit of relationships with friends and family, alone in the city where I lived, so far from you. I felt alone in my health struggles, alone in my faith, alone in the things that brought me the most joy. I felt alone in my soul so that every once in a while, I could feel a little more whole in your arms. Yet, at the end of it all, I do not feel whole. Although I freely gave, I feel used. My giving without regard for my own preferences, made me into an object of gratification that was never enough. I felt you were never happy with just *me*. There was never the approval I desperately craved from you. These feelings keep playing on the screen of my heart, like a movie on a projector screen; your contrasting words as the soundtrack in the background, "I wish you knew how good I treat you."

I am writing this because I think in a few months, I will hear from you, asking me if I am ready to be friends. I do not know what to say. I do not want to be on bad terms because you were so meaningful for such a long time. Yet, I do not like the person you have become or the person I have become to you. A few days after we decided to stop seeing each other, you posted pictures of a date with another girl, the kind of pictures you had never posted of me, even when I was your 'almost fiancé'. If I give you my friendship, allowing you to continue experiencing the connection that exists between us—a connection you have never been able to let go of even when you are dating other women, I feel like a little card being played into your world. A world where I meet your emotional needs while you give all that was supposed to be ours to someone else. A world where there is no value for me. You still call me your soulmate, but the words feel empty, like there is no regard for my actual soul.

I wonder how we got here. I remember when I first met you, you engaged in discussions about

God with curiosity. You were kind. You made me feel seen and known. We bonded over shared values and I was drawn to your unselfishness, humility, and pursuit. I have seen pieces of this in you over the years: your ability to see something's full potential at the time of conception, your choices to improve the way you act in relationships, the humility with which you approach me after disagreements, and your gentleness toward the unlovely and vulnerable. These are beautiful and I thought that was who you were becoming.

When we got back together, you knew what I wanted and said you wanted the same. You engaged me with shared goals and encouraged me in them. Your actions, however, ended up expressing something else. Near the end of our relationship, I told you I was nervous. You were going to a bachelor party and I wanted to avoid another argument about how many drinks you enjoyed; there had been so many of those in the past. When I expressed my concern, you asked me why I was trying to control your life. This was shortly after you asked me why I was not ready to get married.

I remember the time we had the discussion about consciousness. I shared my opinion and you told me I could not have that opinion. This, of course, upset me and the discussion ended with you telling me I picked a fight and feeling angry at how "closed-minded" I was for holding an opinion. I was frequently offending you through simply sharing my heart. I do not know why I tried to keep you for so long. You have become the opposite of what I thought and hoped for. I wanted someone soft, humble, and kind—not someone with whom I would have to live by algorithms.

In trust, I so wholly gave my heart to you. Why does it feel like I completely lost myself to you? I thought losing my heart to yours was the plan. I thought that was what we wanted. So, why does the plan look and feel so much different than I thought it would? Your choice for something different feels like an abandonment of me, of us. When did you stop wanting *us* and our collaborative future? I find myself wondering in the silence of your absence—did you ever truly love me?

It is so confusing to write this because I want to tell you all these things. I want to bleed my hurt over your heart and have you make it okay. I want you to hear and care but that cannot be. The weight of all these questions, all these feelings, all that seems irrecoverably lost, is crushing. So, I feel them all as anger—deep and hot and confusing.

ANGER—GOING FORWARD

How to start over? This is the question I keep

asking myself. I want to run toward a future full of hope, brightness, and good things. I want to be brave enough to do that but I am not sure how to create those things, or even if I can. Seven years of love and care does not fade overnight. It might not ever really go away, but rather, is relearned, reshaped, and replaced by a purer, deeper love for someone else, and maybe also for myself. That is the hardest part—having love in my heart and not having someone to share it with. Having to carry and hold our history on my own. I would like a partner to help me in that: to help me carry the burden, unpack it, forget it or better; use it as a stepping stone toward a shared future. I have wondered: who will love me while pieces of you are still a part of who I am? I also wonder if pieces of you had to become pieces of me so that those pieces of me can be found in whoever is next.

There is a man named Erwin McMannus, who is an incredible speaker in Los Angeles. Today, I listened to his talk entitled, "Choose the Future." He pointed out that sometimes, we are more attracted to the safety of slavery than the uncertainty of freedom. He drew parallels to how this expresses itself in our dating lives and the relationships to which we cyclically return. He explained this phenomenon by saying, "We would rather accept the comfort and safety of a past that holds us captive than the mystery and uncertainty of a future that our souls long for."[1]

All I have ever known is you. I liked that idea for many years since I am a loyal lover. I did not want to deeply love more than one man in my lifetime. It seems unnatural, like swimming with shoes on. Eventually though, I was left holding our love alone, and the weight of love is meant for two. I also think I was a little afraid. Who am I kidding? I have been a lot afraid. Deep down, I have felt unworthy of what my soul truly longs for. I have felt a deep insecurity that no kind, humble, unselfish, patient man will ever love or pick me. Will any man find me the best and most beautiful woman in the world again? Will anyone be attracted to and fall in love with my soul? Most of all, will I be cherished? Will anyone tend to me gently in my weakness like you used to? Who will cry when he looks at me, because of how much I mean to him? Who will love me so much that he likes to just trace my face while I rest? Can I find that in someone who will be gentle, serving, and selfless? Can cherishing and commitment co-exist?

I found the answer in something else from Erwin's message. "If God gave you a new life with the same you, you would ruin that new life, too. You're trapped in the past. You're cycling the same mistakes and the same choices and the same pain and the same fears, over and over and over again."

---

1   McMannus, Erwin, presenter. "The Last Arrow: Choose the future" Mosaic-Erwin McMannus. 15 Oct. 2017. https://itunes.apple.com/us/podcast/mosaic-erwin-mcmanus/id74403741?mt=2

Hearing those words, I knew I had discovered the first step to creating a life that invites the future and the love I desire: it is a new me.

I want to release myself from loving you, so I can find my new self and my future. I want to forgive you for all that went wrong between us. I thank you for loving me to the best of your capacity. I want you to find a loving relationship with someone else, even while my heart is emotionally still arriving at that desire. I believe you are worthy of love and I want you to be happy, healthy, and fulfilled; even without me. Moving forward, I release us, to each find love with someone else. I release us each into the futures our souls long for.

When you and I broke up, I prayed God would give me an early spring in the fall—that He would bring me the life I desire now so I would not have to go through a drawn out waiting period. A few weeks ago, my mom dreamt that she and I visited a church in Australia. The congregation was blowing the horns traditionally used to announce a new season during Jewish new year. When my mother told me about this dream, I felt prompted to look up what season it currently is in Australia. I learned that, in Australia, spring is considered the three *transition* months of September, *October*, and November. Right now, it is October. There I have it—early spring in fall.

Today, I began to think of a caterpillar becoming a butterfly, and molting in general. This is a springtime process, where the old winter coat is shed and the new emerges, ready for the next season. As I reflected, I felt that my spring metamorphosis is happening now, at the same time as my shedding of the old. It is not a loss, pause, gain cycle, but a simultaneous process of the new emerging from the old. In letting you go, I am shedding negative beliefs about the worth of my soul. I am shedding fear that has kept me from fully running into and embracing the future. At the same time, I am also putting on new beliefs about the worth of my soul. I am worthy of being loved and cherished. I have wonderful things that have grown in me, as the result of hardships. I am precious. I have something to offer and I should wait for the best instead of treating myself like a forgotten or unwanted casualty of love.

When we got back together, it seemed everywhere I looked, I found something about springtime rebirth. When we broke up, I felt like we had failed. Instead of being reborn, we broke and died. Maybe, with or without you, there is still a rebirth for me. I have been reborn into new identities, new dreams, and a new future, through the death of us.

This is my dream: I have been thinking about how God's love is wild and reckless, which sounds destructive. But I think in some ways, love is destructive. It destroys expectations: of what your life should look like, of how you should be, of making the right choices. It destroys barriers: of skin color, socioeconomic status, gender, political, or religious views. It destroys barriers of past mistakes. Love destroys every barrier that stands in its way, except for free choice. To me, the ultimate expression of this is the death and resurrection of Christ. To me, wild, reckless love is the gospel. My dream is simply to follow the way of love. Love starts with the unlovely and the individual. So, the first step into my dream is to start loving myself.

LONELY

yle used to say that loneliness meant being alone. I disagreed. However, in the months that followed our breakup, this sometimes felt true. Physically, I was alone quite often. At the time, I was finishing my second year of medical school. The first two years had been filled with housing and health crises that had left me with little time or capacity to cultivate meaningful friendships or a supportive spiritual community. Following the breakup, my roommate was in the process of moving in with her boyfriend. The combination of these factors meant I was often alone in a two-bedroom apartment filled with silence and sadness.

I did not feel the sadness, at first. I remember calling a friend the week that Kyle and I broke up. She asked me how I felt, and I told her I felt fine. She kept telling me that it was okay to be sad, but I kept reassuring her that I was okay. I did not realize I felt panic. The loss was so big, I did not know how to process it. This was equalized by an enormous sense of relief. The burden of trying to untie knots that I had subliminally known for a long time, were not going to work themselves out, was lifted. The effect of these opposing emotions was an anesthetized numbness.

Next, I tried anxiety and agitation, cloaked as hopefulness and longing for the future. I spent a week doing the rebound tour of Bumble, swiping mindlessly through endless profiles, before realizing that it was not at all what my soul wanted. Mostly, though, I felt a franticness to build a new life, find new friends, and experience new things. I wanted my life to feel exciting and full of vibrancy, so I could fool myself into thinking that nothing was lost or missing. I wanted the breakup to yield beauty—the kind found in fireworks and tango music, not introspection and stillness. More than anything, I wanted a new relationship. I thought I was ready. I thought I had loved well in my past relationship and could simply take all the skills I learned there and apply them to someone new. In the early days of my grief, I was unable to visualize my bright, new future without a shiny, new relationship.

As an act of God's grace, there was no shiny new relationship, and the realization of sadness eventually came. It rolled heavily over my heart like dense fog or a wet blanket. In its presence, I felt lonely. I felt the emptiness and absence of losing someone I deeply loved. There were days I longed to "go home," but I could not because home was no longer a relationship with Kyle. There were days when I longed to be held and he was not there to wrap his arms around me. What I could feel was space. Wide, empty, gaping, painful space. It was just me. I discovered in this space that even in loneliness, presence could exist. Presence with God and myself, was the remedy to loneliness when I was alone. Presence looked a little like this:

LONELY

The silence inside my apartment tonight is profound. It sounds like loneliness. Tonight, I am sick in bed. The space inside my bedroom is quiet, dark, and still- untouched by anyone but me. It holds eerie similarities to the emptiness inside my own heart.

Tonight, my roommate is carving pumpkins with her boyfriend. Tonight, the small group I was planning on going to is meeting. Girls are gathering in a dimly lit living room, laughing and bonding over snacks and shared stories. Tonight, I am reading and reflecting, listening to the sound of my breath weaving its way through my body, as it feels like the world is going by without me.

Since Kyle and I broke up, I have been desperately trying to rebuild my life and rebrand myself. I am trying to make new friends as fast as I can, filling my schedule with things that seem good, like serving at church or trying new activities. The rhythm of my life has been a bit like blaring music, like a song you play way too loud when you cannot afford to stop and admit you are tired. It keeps you going, keeps your feet moving.

Tonight, it feels like my whole world has come to a halt. I cannot go to community group or even classes. The music has been turned down and now I hear it. I hear the aching loneliness that has held a steady presence in the background of my life, like a metronome—setting the pace and tone of how my life is playing itself out. Tonight, there is nothing for me to do but reflect and swim inside that inner loneliness I thought I could out dance.

Tonight, my life does not feel especially worthy. At the moment, it is not glamorous or adventurous. It is not productive or impressive. It is not even connected. My life is nothing that would mesmerize Kyle or attract another person to me. In the absence of all those things, I am confronted with the truth that I am un-partnered and I deeply do not want to be. I want to pick up where I left off with Kyle. I want to jump into the ring and the dress, the apartment and the Saturday morning softness with someone else. I do not want to do this alone—this cold, empty, austerity that is tonight, that is my life right now.

Life has caught up to me with this illness, and all my best attempts to slap together a shiny new life are unraveling and with them, so is a dynamic I learned with Kyle. Love from Kyle felt tied to being enough, a result of striving for that perfect combination of beautiful, intelligent, entertaining, sexy, and funny. His love came from me being something other than myself. It reminds me of how I feel when I drive past his neighborhood in Los Angeles now. It is a swanky area near the beach. Everything there is smooth, slick, and expensive. When I drive through it, it feels cold. It reminds me of shrink-wrapped chicken breast in the refrigerator case at the grocery store: sterile and disconnected from the source, from its natural way of being.

Tonight, I laid in bed. No makeup, no television, no music, no other people. I read an article written by a researcher named Brené Brown. I thought I was going to read about attracting the love you desire or some "change your life" formula, but the article was actually about worthiness. She wrote about the people she studied who were experiencing the most fulfilling lives and relationships; they all deeply believe they are worthy of love and that belief demonstrates itself in *how* they live. Through boundaries and actions of creativity and playfulness, these people know how to move toward themselves in love.[1]

When I read that, I realized I had thought I wanted to be the type of woman Kyle said I needed to be—the strong and beautiful woman who has it all together; the shiny woman who has something to offer. Here in the silence, I can feel my breath under my ribs. My skin feels especially soft, with nothing on it to make me beautiful, and I realize I do not want to be that woman. I do not want to be shrink-wrapped chicken. I want to be *fragile and human*, and I want to be loved in that.

I want to treat myself like I am worthy of

1   (Doable) Ways to Increase the Love in Your Life. (n.d.). Retrieved from http://www.oprah.com/omagazine/how-to-increase-the-love-in-your-life-brene-brown/all

someone who believes that the person I am right now is enough, even in stillness and sickness. In striving for perfection, I have been violating my truest desire for someone who will love and nurture me despite insufficiency. What I truly want is not someone who will love the ideal me, but someone who will pause and love me where I am at. I want someone who will partner with me in the action of moving toward myself in love and who will help me hold witness that I am enough, as I am, right now.

Perhaps one of the reasons I feel so lonely is because I have not loved *myself* in that way. I have been trying to exist unpartnered from my own self. The reason Brené's article was so profound for me was because it illustrated how the people who have what I want, who have exciting lives and connected relationships, do the opposite of what I have been doing. They love *themselves*. They set boundaries in their lives. I see now, in my desperate desire for someone to love me, I am left with no choice but to love myself.

There is something so much more alive about being fragile than being perfect, about being broken than unbreakable. It hurts a little because I feel and see more, but I am alive. There is something about realness that is like breath. It moves in unforced rhythms, which is so different from the frantic dance of perfection with which I have been trying to keep pace.

I have been so desperately trying to create a

new life that I forgot something: the only reason I can create is because God made me to and the only way to create the future I desire is to dance in partnership with Him. I have thought that I needed to do copious activities and avoid isolation to be worthy of meaningful relationships. While neither isolation or idleness are positive states of existence, the message I have been operating from is that I have to labor, be strategic and be seen, to earn meaningful relationships and build a meaningful future. Yet, none of the most wonderful things in my life have come through strategy, or white knuckling, or refusing to rest. They have come through divinely opened doors—like a last-minute university application becoming my Ivy League Alma Mater, like some stranger in a coffee shop becoming the person I loved most. All of these beginnings were not from my own effort, and I feel God reminding me of that tonight. New beginnings will not come from me striving to become the perfect person, finding the perfect partner, or building the perfect life. It will come from God's creative direction that moves through grace, rest, and a deeply rooted knowing of self-worth.

So, I am leaning into this moment, embracing the fact that I am sick because right now, it is teaching me. Without it, I would forget to guard my heart. I would chase after who I think I should be instead of perhaps, who God actually made me to be. Maybe, when I have learned to place boundaries on my life to protect my heart, to lavish myself with rest, sickness will be ready to leave, and the future I desire will arrive. Tonight, as I lay around at home, I have to remind myself that this is the time to really live out the belief that I am worthy. Tonight, when nobody sees or notices me, or is buying me a pumpkin. Tonight, when I cannot go to my small group or serve at church, I AM WORTHY. I breathe in, pause, then exhale: I BELONG TO GOD. I AM SEEN.

Loneliness has always made me feel like something is wrong with me. I have let it be the voice of imperfection, highlighting my flaws. It has been the internal critic of what is, measuring against what should be. I have felt lonely because I feel like I should be doing something else, like I should have plans or someone to share my plans with me. For far too long, I have let loneliness comment on my worth. Tonight, that is changing. Tonight, loneliness is becoming a warm light that illuminates my humanness, my aliveness. Tonight, I took care of myself as a single human being and there is nothing wrong with that. Loneliness does not mean there is something intrinsically wrong with me or my life. It simply means I am human, and I desire connection; both of which are normal and healthy.

I feel the way one does when the sun illuminates your skin and it seems to glow. It lights up freckles and scars—everything is more visible but everything is more beautiful because it is so real. Tonight, I see the reality that I am single and alone. In the same warm light, I see that it is okay to be single and happy. It is okay to be me and to be fully alive when I feel unseen. It is okay to appreciate the ways others do see me. I am not putting on a show for love anymore. I am breathing and existing in all my glorious fragility, in all my heartbreaking but healing loneliness. And it is okay to be at peace knowing no human being can ever perfectly or completely fill my longing to be seen. I am remembering that God is the partner who loves me just the way I am, who covers me just the way that I am. He blesses me in my insufficiency, just the way that I am. No dancing, no performing. Just breathing, just receiving.

This is my declaration for myself—my intention for my life and love letter to myself:

I am a daughter of God, even when I do not feel like it
I am full of life, even when I cannot get out of bed
I was made for, am worthy of, and can contribute to a relationship, even when I am alone
I can serve God, even when I am too tired for activity

I am willing to go slow, to live a life that is unglamorous and unadventurous
because that is where I am at right now
because I want to live a life of love

And right now, being willing to love myself in obscurity is inviting the love I want.

Here is what I have learned about being alone: from loneliness comes presence; from rejection comes worth. This is important because in the silence of grief, loneliness likes to make comments about your value. What I learned is that bringing presence to loneliness was one of the most significant processes of grief. By letting myself embrace the loneliness, leaning into it, and experiencing how it felt in all its nuances, I lived a new truth. I lived a quiet, rebellious declaration that I am worthy of love in that silent, unseen, unimportant, lonely place. It became a discipline that looked different every time but that I always returned to. Through this process, in some strange way, loneliness helped me learn to feel less alone.

SOUL FRIENDS

FOR JONNY & BETHANY, TIM & NICOLE,
AMY, ALLI, BRI, AND SARAH

When I lost Kyle, I felt disconnected. I had a network of friends in San Diego but one that extended wide, rather than deep. The deep friends that I did have were spread wide across the country, accessible only by phone. As much as I did not know how to build a new life, I knew that I needed deeper community. And so, I went to church. I possessed deep church anxiety because church people had mostly been harsh, degrading, exclusive, and abusive toward me. I felt like I did not really belong at church, but I wrote this prayer and went anyway, with a hope for something different:

November 2017

FRIENDSHIP

Today, I am struggling with the state of loneliness in which I currently exist. Today, I listened to three sermons and all talked about how we need community. I did not overlook the irony of listening to something intended for a communal setting in complete isolation. I have not had community in a long time, and I am wondering: what does community even look like for me?

I know what I have wanted it to look like: romantic relationship. For a long time, Kyle was a substitute for community in my life. Since I lost him, I have been longing for someone to build community with, in place of Kyle. I have also been thinking sometimes the community God sends us does not look the way we expect it to. I sense God wants something different for me in this new season. Relationship with Kyle was both more and less vulnerable than friendship: more vulnerable because of the depths to which I loved him, but less vulnerable because I knew he loved me. Being in a relationship with him did not require the same awkward risk of rejection that one feels when showing up to a church potluck or attending an event with a room full of strangers; wondering if they think I am weird or ugly. I do not think God wants my next love to be a replacement for community or a detour around vulnerability, but rather a connection to both. I believe a new romantic relationship will carry the purpose of creating a generative community that can be shared with others in a nourishing way, like a hot meal. I have wondered if during this time God wants me to focus on building friendships, while waiting for Him to bring a new partner to me in His time.

So, I have concluded that I need friends, but not just any friends. I am hungry for spiritual connection and community. I am praying God would send me

SOUL friends—friends I would experience growth with and who will sow into my spirit.

Recently, my friend wrote me these words, "Chelsea, good friends are coming. He will send good people who will be your spiritual friends. His love for you will be very real in the coming season."

The soul friends did come. Long before I wrote that letter, when I first moved to San Diego, I started sporadically attending a church. I loved it because they had a woman pastor, pastors who wore skinny jeans, and many young people who worshipped through poetry as well as music. I loved it because you had to walk past rows and rows of homeless tents to get inside and sometimes the homeless would wander in and listen to the music. Later the church moved to a theater and we sang to God beneath red, velvet curtains. I never planned to leave, but I did. A few years later, after I had written my reflection on friendship, I laid in bed one Saturday morning, scrolling through social media. There was a pastor from Los Angeles, whose story I followed. Kyle had introduced me to him because he had a chronically sick daughter, who reminded Kyle of me. Later, when I lost Kyle, I read this pastor's book called *Unreasonable Hope*. That particular Saturday morning, he had posted an old family photo and tagged his sister. One thing led to another and soon, I was scrolling through her profile. I discovered that she and her husband had a church in San Diego, one that I had heard of before. Something inside me was curious, so the next day, I got up and attended their church. I do not remember what the message was. It did not overly wow or inspire me. However, I could not shake the idea of trying a small group there. So, I did. At the first gathering I attended, I met the pastor and his wife. There was something about their souls that was beautiful. They were so humble, friendly, and down to earth. I felt like I might be welcome in this community. As I drove to this first gathering, I thought about divinely opened doors, and afterward I wrote this letter:

November 2017

DOORS OF HOPE

Tonight, on my way to small group, I prayed about doors. Song has been talking about God opening doors of destiny and I have felt a knowing that these doors are somehow opening for me.

Tonight, I walked through the Wonder's front door with a paper bag full of kombucha and chocolate covered goji berries to share. In a quiet way, it felt like walking into a new season of life. Since breaking up with Kyle, life has looked like the inside of my apartment. My apartment has two bay windows on the eastern side that allow the darkness of nightfall to creep inside unrestrained. This season of life has tasted like the salty tears that flow even more unrestrained. Life has sounded like the podcasts I listen to on repeat to help me forget my loneliness, like memories washing themselves out of my heart through my emotions and often, like the silence created by no one stirring inside my home but myself. The inside of the Wonder's home could not be more opposite. It was alive with people: children running in and out of the main living areas, dads playing with them while chatting to each other, women talking while stirring pots of soup and arranging baskets of sliced bread. We gathered around a long, rectangular table for dinner. I talked and I listened to others talk. After dinner, we sat in a circle, discussing the Bible and how God speaks to everyone, even to people who do not know Him. Before I left, I helped wash dishes while telling the pastor's wife about my schooling, as if it was my kitchen, my home, my family.

What tonight felt like was community. It reminded me of all the ways God cultivates tangible community with His people in the scriptures. In ancient times, when the primary method of connecting with God was visiting His tabernacle tent, He instructed His priests to keep fresh baked bread in a part of the tent that was close to His presence. The bread acted as a sign of friendship to His people. It represented a desire for intimacy with them, much like you would experience over a meal in the kitchen of someone who loved you. The night before Jesus went to the cross, He ate bread and drank wine with His followers. When He rose from the grave, He cooked breakfast for them on the beach. I sometimes think God is a little like an Italian mother saying "Eat, eat! Come eat in my kitchen!" God's table is surrounded with His people, set with His blessings, and has a way, through both connection and food, of feeding your soul. Tonight, I felt like I was invited back to that table—a table that for so long has felt like the exclusive table in the Jr. High lunchroom more than God's welcoming table of friendship.

On my way home from small group, I thought it was funny how without Kyle, I would not have been at that meeting tonight, the meeting where I felt so much warmth and acceptance. Kyle introduced me to the pastor who introduced me to this church. On Rosh Hashanah, I listened to a sermon given by the pastor Kyle introduced me to. Rosh Hashanah was the first day of my new era but, as the same day Kyle and I had selected for our wedding, it was also a difficult day. The sermon was about this Bible verse "(I) will make Trouble Valley a *door* of hope."[1] I am learning that hope is not a single door, but rather a series of them. I think another door of hope opened for me tonight, when I attended this new small group. From Kyle, my place of disappointment,

---

1   Hosea 2:15 Good News Translation

a door opened into my destiny of hope.

So, I kept going—both to the Sunday morning gatherings and the small group. On Sundays, the pastor and his wife would stand on the stage and say that this was a place where you could belong, before you believed. I had believed for a long time, but for the first time in my life I felt like I belonged in church. At first, I would arrive late to the services and leave immediately after, to avoid the possibility of having no one to talk to. Something amazing pulled me out of that. The people who made me feel like I belonged also believed in me. They saw my gifts and talents, called out life in me, and made me feel like a valued part of the community. They gave me hope for my future. The name of this little church was Soul Church and the people at this place were not just my friends. They were exactly what I had asked God for: **SOUL** friends.

FEELINGS

As I moved through grief, I learned that it was not the only feeling in the process of moving forward. Grieving felt a lot like being "hormonal," but all the time, instead of for just one week—one moment you are irritable at nothing at all, the next you feel so happy you might pop, the next that happiness has bubbled its way into deep sadness and hysterical tears. At the end of the day, you still do not know how to feel, so you are just tired. In my grieving, it was often easier to feel nothing at all. I wrote this letter in a moment when I first started to realize that I could unpack grief into all its separate components and I could feel each one.

Learning to feel was a lot like coming up for air, after floating in a sea of numbness. The feelings were like oxygen, filling me with life and empowering me to swim, just a little further, giving me what I needed to make it to the next breath. In the same stroke, feeling them burned a little. Emotional numbness had helped me ignore the fact that, instead of living the life I wanted, I was living life as usual. I was focused on the externals of building a new life and feeling forced me to focus on the internal processes. Unpacking feelings did not seem like anything significant. Yet, beneath the surface of my haze of emotions, there was enough activity in my heart to write a book. Or at least a letter.

November 2017

FEELINGS

The past week has been full of emotions: grief, doubt, excitement, exhaustion. It seemed all these emotions stacked up in my heart, until yesterday, they burst. Or maybe it was my heart that burst under the weight of the emotions. The girl who spoke at my women's small group shared a story similar to mine and it broke me. I felt loss and sadness, confusion, and hurt all over again. I felt the enormity of living a broken life. I felt uncomfortable.

I felt uncomfortable because I have been running from the fact that emotionally, I am not okay. My heart is fractured and hurting, even when I try to pretend otherwise. Loss of Kyle took a toll on my faith, hope, and optimism. Right now I live struggling to believe that God is good and that there is hope for the future. Last night, those feelings confronted me in the face, reminding me that they are too important to be ignored.

As I drove home from group yesterday, I kept remembering a song I have been listening to where the singer talks about Jesus' dead friend Lazarus, who was resurrected from the grave. In this story, Jesus, knowing He was going to call His friend out from the clutch of death, paused to weep. In the singer's retelling of the story, she points out that Jesus Himself leans into the human process of grief. Even knowing the ending, He does not skip the process of experiencing the feelings the present situation demands. In doing so, He elevates our feelings. He dignifies them to something beyond the ashes we feel them to be. He brings the spiritual from the physical, like life from the grave, and in feeling, unites the two. Remembering this song and the perspectives it brought, I felt perhaps, all the things building up in the week were God's way of reminding me to acknowledge that I am hurt and saddened by Kyle. It felt like God was saying that He was grieving with me.

So, I allow myself to feel the hurt. I feel hurt that Kyle did not choose me, and that there were things he wanted more than trying to make things work with me. I am sad because I feel like I lost the Kyle I fell in love with. I feel sad that so much of me was also lost with him. I am saddened and afraid that I may have wasted seven years of my life investing the most precious resource I have.—my heart, into something that failed and broke me in the process. I felt this acutely when I attended a co-ed community church group earlier in the week. It triggered an exaggerated sense of starting over, like I was shopping leftovers. As I sat with this sadness, a verse came to mind—"you prepare a table before me in the presence of my enemies."[1] With that, I knew my heart was not the scraps I felt my life to be. I am a treasure. I spent seven years learning to love well, and time spent learning to love is not wasted in the least.

It is now the month of November, a time when harvest festivals are followed by the Thanksgiving table: a symbol of abundance. I believe that is the spiritual table God is preparing for me. I am not shopping leftovers. I get to eat from the bountiful Thanksgiving table—a table that was prepared for me through faithfulness in love and loss.

In this month, though I feel hurt, there is also peace knowing Kyle and I are over and I get a fresh start. As I feel each one of my emotions, I am setting the table. I acknowledge grief, anger, or abandonment—the emotion du jour—wringing the sadness out of it and it is over. I am fresh. I have rest. From this mess of emotions, God is creating beauty and bounty.

1   Psalm 23:5 New International Version

WONDER

hen I first started playing with the idea of switching to Soul Church, the word "wonder" was stuck in my head. It was as if someone had written the word in neon inside my brain. One morning, I was listening to a song called *Wonder*,[1] and I said, "God, I can't get this word *wonder* out of my head." Immediately after having that thought, I opened my phone to the webpage with a list of the community groups available to join at the new church. The very first group I saw was hosted by a couple named the Wonders. It just so happened this was the only group that I could attend, due to my schedule. So, this was the group I showed up to week after week. The group was wonderful and warm. We met on Friday nights for community dinner and visiting. The only problem with it was that I was the only single person in the group. It was composed of couples, and most of the couples had children. Coming fresh out of a relationship that was supposed to have ended in us becoming a family, I felt excruciatingly awkward attending. I often felt like the group members would wonder why I came to a

---

1   "Wonder", by Hillsong

couple's group, or why I did not have anything better to do on a Friday night than eat dinner with married parents.

Nevertheless, I needed a deeper community, so I kept going. I would give myself little pep talks in my car about how my worth and ability to connect with other adults was not derived from my marital status—I had value to offer regardless of the fact I brought no family. It was there, at the Wonders' dinner table, with screaming children in the background, that my heart began to shift. I started to realize that a life of wonder was unfolding out of my grief. This group gave me the first few glimpses of a future more brilliant than my past, and it helped me to set my intention for that future.

November 2017

A PARTNER IN WONDER

I cannot seem to get away from this word: wonder. I have been meditating on the idea of living a life of wonder; of further discovering the way God's beauty softens us and His mystery unravels us. I have a hunger to chase God's beauty and life, allowing it to bring me into deeper and delighted astonishment of Him. Wonder so incredibly describes this paradox that the more we discover, the deeper the mystery becomes, but it is not a mystery of confusion. It is one that enlightens, deepens intimacy, and pulls us into greater joy and delight.

Tonight, I sat at the Wonder's dinner table,

listening to each couple tell their "how we met" story and as I listened, I felt a prayer in my heart go up to God. I asked for God to send someone to share these experiences with. Tonight, maybe for the first time since losing Kyle, this prayer came not from a place of loneliness or discontent or low worth. Rather, it came from a recognition of *wonder.* I heard a story the other day about a man describing the way he decided to propose to his wife. He was standing on cliffs overlooking Newport and Laguna beaches, and it was one of the most beautiful things he had ever seen in his life. This beauty led him to realize that he desired someone to share it with. His realization came from a moment of fullness and breathtaking beauty—not one of lack or pain.

That is how I felt—not like I am looking for someone to fill my holes —I feel God doing that, but rather for someone to share life's fullness with me. I feel like I am receiving new waves of God— waves of His beauty and love. I feel as if I am standing at the edge of something breathtaking, gazing at God's glory, and I want someone to share it with. I want someone whose hand I can hold, and together we can dive into this experience of living a life of wonder; beholding and discovering God's beauty together, amplifying it for each other. I want to be with someone who carries wonder inside of them. I want to have a partner who will expand my capacity to run into marvel, adventure, and the "great unknown". I want to be with someone who, in the words of Mary Oliver, is the "bridegroom taking the world into (his) arms", and I the "bride married to amazement."[2] Tonight, I thought it was funny that God led me to this married group—the Wonder's group. Maybe this is a promise, a shadow of things coming, acknowledging that God is answering my heart's prayer before I fully formed it.

I listened to a message recently titled Set Your Past on Fire.[3] The thing about wonder is that it calls you to do as the message is titled—to set your past on fire. If you want to step into a beautiful, mysterious dance with the future, you cannot carry your clunky past with you. Wonder also calls you to set your present on fire, to be fully alive in the moment. Setting the past on fire is this gory, destructive, extreme end to everything in the past. It leaves only ashes. Setting the present on fire is about finding what makes you feel alive. What sets your heart on fire? What illuminates your life with blazing, golden, glory and warmth and energy and excitement? What fills you with a sense of wonder?

I feel like both setting my past and present on fire are simultaneously happening in my life. In the tension between the two, there is mystery and wonder. There are little pieces of my heart

---

2   Mary Oliver's poem, "When Death Comes"

3   McMannus, Erwin, presenter. "The Last Arrow: Set Your Past on Fire." Mosaic-Erwin McMannus. 22 Oct. 2017. https://itunes.apple.com/us/podcast/mosaic-erwin-mcmanus/id74403741?mt=2

arranging themselves back together and I receive it in amazement.

PATIENCE

The night Kyle and I got back together before our final breakup, we spoke over the phone since he was living in Las Vegas. At the end of the call, he told me he needed to think about things—about us, before making a decision to get back together. A few minutes after we hung up, my phone lit up with a text from him, "I love you. And I miss you. And I've missed telling you I love you. I'm ready to be home."

I wanted to wrap myself inside the exhilaration I felt, that my phone was again vibrating with words from him. It felt like home, like my heart was realigned, where it belonged. I wrote back a long declaration of how humbled I was that he would let his heart be home to me, and of how much I missed him. It began with the words "you melt me."

The winter after our final breakup, I found myself wanting to melt into Kyle, or into someone else. I wanted my soul to again fit with another, to hear words of warmth that would soften my icy soul: the soul was hurt, sad, and angry, forgetting what the sunshine of tenderness felt like. I had dreaded this winter. If fall was letting go, winter was what fall let go into. Stillness that feels like death.

One year later, I transcribed this letter. As I typed, it was sunny and warm, and the stillness of winter felt like peaceful rest. I think this is because I let my heart go underground. I let it be enveloped by the season. This work formed the process of patience. Patience is sitting in the moment with everything you want and what you actually have. Patience is finding, in winter, the ingredients of a new season.

December 2017

WINTER

I remember the first time I visited New York City. I was in college at the time and couldn't afford the pricy plane ticket home for the Thanksgiving weekend. So I took a bus to Manhattan to stay with a friend in her studio apartment. I had always wanted to be in Manhattan at Christmastime. The day after Thanksgiving, we bundled up in our coats and scarves to see the Christmas lights on 5th Ave. There was Cartier wrapped in giant red ribbons and Bergdorf Goodman with icy blue snowflake lights hanging in the windows. We walked past The Plaza Hotel, where Kevin stays in the movie *Home Alone*, and we ended with a walk in Central Park, where the trees were still wearing leaves in golden hues. The experience was rich and full but it felt empty without Kyle.

Kyle looked out for me in a special way when I was in college. When I first moved across the country (from California to New York), I called him everyday. I called him crying the first time I got a bad grade on a test and when I walked home from classes. The first long weekend I had, he flew me home because he knew I was homesick for him and my family. We loved each other back then, even though we were pretending to just be friends. Later, when we dropped the friends act and started dating, he would send me care packages with things he had heard me mention I needed as well as luxuries like expensive jewelry, articles of clothing sprayed in his cologne, and love notes. A few months before my Thanksgiving trip to Manhattan, I had been saving to take Kyle there to express my gratitude for his care for me. Kyle loved everything sophisticated and I knew he would love it there. It would be an adventure just for us; I was even saving to take him to a fancy restaurant.

Before I could plan the trip, we were broken up, again. I don't remember the real reason we broke up but a few weeks before this, we had been fighting about him eating at McDonald's and this breakup was infamously and humorously named "the McDonald's breakup", by our friends. When I was in Manhattan, I kept thinking, *"Kyle would love this"* and *"I wish Kyle could see this."* Although it was Christmas, and I was surrounded by warmth and cheer, it felt more like winter—empty and cold.

That is what this year has felt like. Winter. And, I am aching for it to be spring. The word patience has been on my mind of late. God is patient. Love is patient. I have been meditating on this poetic passage of scripture about seasons of waiting calling for patience, "Write down the vision; make it plain on tablets, so he may run who reads it. For still the vision awaits its appointed time; it hastens to the end—it will not lie. If it seems slow, wait for it; it will surely come; it will not delay." These words are basically saying to keep in mind the vision for the future that has been revealed to you. When it feels like that vision will never come to pass, use this remembrance to persevere. I have been encouraged, by these words, that I can wait with patience for the unseen 'new'. The longings of my heart foreshadow that there is a greater measure of love and healing for me that *will* arrive at their appointed time.

The words of this scripture are dynamic; they are words about writing and running, things associated with forward motion. Yet these dynamic words also speak of patience and waiting. They demonstrate that there is power in patience. I have been singing a song called *Seasons* which describes promises as seeds that must go underground to get through winter and grow. It talks of the hardship of winter, and how the longer this season stretches, the richer the harvest we can expect. It reminds us how God almost always works in seasons, in slow intentional work, like sending His son as a baby in a manger who would grow into the Savior on the cross. Like the scripture verse that speaks of forward motion through patient waiting, the words of this song speak of stillness and momentum contained in the same season—winter.

Yesterday, I prayed about how desperately I am craving a season change. I was driving in the car. The sun was shining through the window, its warmth contrasting the hollow feeling in my bones, and I heard God whisper *"Ice."* Not the word I wanted to hear. When I lived in New York, I lived near a lake. I walked past waterfalls to get to class, and during the winter, the waterfalls would freeze into spectacular displays of icicles, suspended over the sides of the rocks. *Ice*—dynamic motion frozen to a standstill.

Last night after I prayed this, I had a dream that I was visiting somewhere snowy but I was dressed for spring. I was there for a wedding but it was taking a long time to start and I was growing restless. Noticing my boredom, a friend who was traveling with me convinced me to go outside and explore some nearby ice caves. I agreed. We went outside and as soon as I set foot in the cave, it melted. I was unharmed but a little disgruntled that I had to change my clothes.

This morning, I listened to the song *Seasons* about ten times on my drive to school and wept. Not the pretty, gentle weeping. The ugly kind—where you are heaving and whaling in your car while tears wash mascara down your cheeks. I wept because I realized the invitation of my life right now is not to spring. It is to winter. As I reflected on what God might mean by telling me this was a season of "ice", these thoughts rolled into my head *"Ice. Winter. A time of silence when things are happening underground that appear dead above ground. A time when everything is buried deep in the earth and seems mostly forgotten."* With these words, I began to understand ice and winter in a new way. Ice looks like death but beneath the surface is brilliant life. In its season, ice melts and all that has been restrained beneath comes crashing through, shattering icicles into a thousand tiny crystals. Ice, like patience, is the symbol that dormant is not dead. Hope delayed is not hope lost.

Today, I wept because I do not yet feel the shifting these impressions speak of. The intensity with which I feel my life freezing, condensing, and withdrawing—its heartbeat slowing to a nearly dead pulse, is painful. It reminds me of stepping outside on a winter day to a cold so severe, it deadens all your other senses. Yet, as I sang *Seasons*, I also wept because I realized that I can transform winter with patience. In my dream, winter did not begin to melt until I embraced the season of waiting and opened my heart to exploring the wonder of it. After the ice melted, my clothes were changed, which I think represents *myself* and the way I present myself to the world being changed, being transformed into a readiness for what is next.

Likewise in my life, I do not think winter will begin to melt until I *engage* with it, until I cultivate it. My engagement with this season, through patience, is part of my process of transformation. As I allow my heart to submerge into the grinding halt, I am able to discover the tiniest treasures of the season in intricate detail, as if I were studying a single, breathtaking snowflake. As I find beauty in this season, I understand that there is more to be learned in winter—there are things, people, and partnerships to explore.

Patience is not hibernation. It is transformation. It is an invitation to come out and play, to be an ice queen, taking dominion over winter and transforming her into something exquisite as my own Father does, over and over again, year after year, season after season.

In my winter of grief I grew, and patience grew. I learned how life can be beautiful while being still. A few winters later, I can look back and say change has come and is still coming. Patience was not just power, courage or stillness and growth. Patience was preparation. In patience, I discovered this truth:

"Do you hear nothing?
silence too will speak, if you will listen
she says 'there is enough noise

awaiting you. for now, peace.'"[1]
T.R.

---

1   T.R.H. From "Go & Listen to the Morning" www.notesontheway.
com Used with permission

SINGLE

This morning I went to church and learned that another couple who attend there got engaged. In the past year, handfuls of single people at my small church have begun serious relationships or become engaged—people who thought it would never happen for them, or were not looking for it. This weekend one of my girlfriends, who lost the love of her life this year, is at a ski retreat. She is surrounded by couples, PDA, and feelings of grief. This same weekend a girl I know from high school had her second baby. I am surrounded by life moving forward.

Something strange has happened to me. I find myself moving forward as well, moving on from Kyle. I have mostly forgotten what it is like to live in a partnership, having my heart adored, pursued, and opened by tenderness. I have learned how to be happy, how to take care of myself, and how to cultivate relationships without a partner. I have learned how to be whole on my own. I have learned how to be single, and how to be single gracefully and well.

Yet sometimes, there are moments, like those this weekend, when life feels a little incomplete. You realize that people are moving on, and having babies, and growing up. Others, like my girlfriend and I, are growing and expanding in other ways within our hearts. Mostly, this is fulfilling. Sometimes though, it carries a sense of loss. In losing Kyle, I did not just lose Kyle. I felt like I had lost my opportunity to begin my journey of motherhood, to build the community of a family, and to expand and grow in partnership with another heart. I lost the ability to discover the depths of my soul, inside my love for another person. I am still waiting for those things to be recovered.

Singleness is not just your relational status. It is a challenge requiring a fierce sense of self and an undying devotion to optimism. It calls you to inhabit the present while maintaining a commitment to your belief in a restored future. There are moments, like this weekend, when you want to give up believing in that future, or when you want to create a future now, even if that means compromising for a love much less than you know you are worthy of.

Singleness is one of the beginning steps to a wild heart. It is full of risk and bravery, gambling your heart on your dreams. As much as I was committed to Kyle, I have learned to be committed to the belief that I am worthy of waiting for a healthy relationship. This letter is about going forward while single, which I learned is very different from going forward alone.

December 2017

SINGLENESS

A few Sundays ago, we read the love chapter at church. You know the, "Love is patient, Love is kind"[1] one. We read it through replacing the word love with the word God, and I heard something spectacular in it, "God does not insist on His own way." Maybe it is because Kyle was so controlling that I found this so revelatory, but from that moment on I have lived in this wondrous realization that God invites me into His creative process. He is not forcing me to achieve a certain outcome; He is simply loving me to freely discover the best He has for me. Through the interaction of my choice with His heart and desires for me, we get to craft something beautiful, forming part of the story of how I come alive.

I was recently reminded that a key step to creating a beautiful life with God, is making the decision to persevere past fears. My life is littered with reminders that the future is almost always just on the other side of your fears. If I am honest, lately I have been facing the temptation to stop short in life. I have felt like I have waited enough. I just want to be with anyone, and be done with grief. Or more accurately, be done with singleness. This decision would be easy and normal. It is a decision so many people make after loss, especially that of a romantic partner. But, extraordinary futures are

---

1   1 Corinthians 13 New International Version

not made by ordinary decisions. They are made by pushing past the point where others have stopped short in life. They are made by believing there is more than what is right here and right now. Today, I felt God's gentle invitation to take hold of the "more" in life by going further in my process and deeper in my waiting.

I remember times when Kyle told me he would not love me if I did not grow in ways he deemed acceptable. God's challenge to growth is not like that; "God does not insist on His own way." I do not have to go further and deeper than I am right now. God will love me just the same either way. Today I thought of a story in the Bible about David, one of the most famous kings in all Bible history, who was a great warrior. One day he came back to his camp after being defeated in a battle, only to find that his camp had been set on fire and his family kidnapped. I thought of David's devastation in the face of losing his family and the family of his band of outcast men. There is a phrase in this story that stands in contrast to its tones of despair, "David strengthened himself in the Lord his God, to pursue and overtake those who had stolen from him."[2] I feel a similar call in my life right now: a call to make a choice, but not from loss, discouragement, despair, or even obligation. I feel a call to make a choice unhindered by those things—a call to push

---

2   1 Samuel 30:6 New International Version

past disheartened grief, believing there is a future so victorious, it will be as if nothing was ever lost. This is a call fueled by love that cannot create anything but more love.

The future, however, is built one tiny step at a time. It is built by taking step after step to embrace the singleness that lies between me and the extraordinary ending to my story of heartbreak. Today, this tiny step looked like building community so I do not feel lonely, whether I have a partner or not. In this action, I felt myself one step closer to becoming the wild-hearted woman I want to be: a woman who is brave and confident, doing things that feel uncomfortable and vulnerable to claim my power and live in truth. Another tiny step was making the choice, *again*, to allow myself to have worth independent of a partner, a choice which is preparing my heart for the blessings God is sending me. If I received those blessings before learning to love myself, I could not experience them to their fullest.

I recently heard someone propose that bold futures do not come by simply moving forward; they require us to say, "NO!" to a lesser future. This idea reminds me of other words from the Scriptures that prescribe an affirmation, "We are not those who shrink back in fear."[3] If I am co-creating with God, there is no room for fear in the equation. There is

---

3   Hebrews 10:39

only room for love. There is only room to discover myself and my future inside His love for me. So, I want to say to God that I am not going to stay behind. I am not going to settle for any relationship or life circumstance that is easy and complacent. I am not going to miss out on my future because of fear. I am going to embrace singleness while I keep hoping audaciously and saying yes to life. In a million small ways. In ways that I fear. In faith, knowing my tiny decisions today are painting, in broad brushstrokes, the brilliant future of tomorrow. And, I want to say to myself:

I give myself permission to be single.
I will not wear this like a badge of shame.
I will not listen when it tries to tell me lies about my worth, my normalcy, my beauty, or my attractiveness.
I will make friends with singleness. I will wear her proudly and bravely.
She is not my identity, but she compliments my identity.
She allows my neglected places to be warmed with love and my most beautiful parts to be seen. She allows me to stop wasting time listening to the voices of my past and give myself wholeheartedly to my present.
I give myself permission to love myself, to have patience with my process, to see myself as whole, loved, valuable, and contributing—NOW, just as I am.
I allow myself to discover a beautiful and amazing future now.

I allow myself to see the beauty and amazement in singleness.

The first few years following my breakup with Kyle, whenever my friends asked me how I felt about singleness and if I wanted to date again, I almost always responded by telling them about a man who made an impression on me, after the breakup. He was tall with big blue eyes and an impressive resume. He shared my field of work, and gave me a lot of attention. One day, we found ourselves alone and talking about many things, one of them being dating in general. After that conversation, I thought about whether I would be interested in him romantically. When I thought about what I liked about him, I realized I liked the way he made me feel when I was around him. I liked that he made me feel smart, pretty, and seen. None of those are bad things and may very well be a good foundation when getting to know another person more deeply. Yet, they caused me to realize if I ever get back into a relationship, I do not want those to be the reasons why. I want to get back into a relationship because I deeply admire and respect the other person, because I am captivated by his vision for life and find myself aligned with the same vision. Until and unless I find that in someone who also feels the same way about me, I have learned to be unafraid of going forward single and un-alone.

BROKEN HEART

The very first time Kyle and I ever talked about dating, we were just kids. I was barely nineteen and he was only a few years older. I came to the conversation with much trepidation, wondering how to voice the fact that I wanted to date him seriously without sounding clingy or needy. He came to the conversation with intention. He looked at me with those big blue eyes and told me that he was going to marry me. Seven years later, we sat in a jewelry store and held hands while I tried on a 3-carat diamond ring. Together, we had solved a string of logistical problems: rearranging our lives, homes, and careers in preparation for a proposal.

One such problem was the selection of an apartment, where Kyle would live until we married. The week before his move, we fought a lot. We fought about the choices each of us was making and who each of us was becoming, though these issues were cloaked in much more shallow arguments. We fought because another girl had kissed him, and I wanted him to stop talking to her and following her on social media. This was yet another way he found me negative and he was tired of hearing what I thought was wrong with the relationship. The week of the move was supposed to be better. Kyle had left the new apartment unfurnished to be filled with my furniture, in preparation for our marriage. Since there was nothing to sit on, we sat on the floor and fought. Then kissed. Then fought. Then kissed—over and over, like a dramatic scene from a bad movie.

The same week, the seams that had been splitting for a long time began to unravel. In between the moving and cuddling, the kissing and fighting, the talks about who we were and where we were going—we found ourselves to be two different people. We did not want the same things anymore. We did not believe the same things anymore. Initially, this did not come as a shock since he had been formulating what he fundamentally believed the entire time I had known him. He kept shifting his beliefs, splitting from them and rejoining them. I thought this time Kyle's changing beliefs were because he was nervous or scared, or working through something and we would realign. We did not. This was the week that I lost his heart and he lost mine. From that week on, he changed in a way I had never seen him change before. He became another person, someone totally different than the man I had loved for seven years. I kept trying to keep our relationship going because I had loved him for so long I thought relational CPR might be possible. I tried because so many dreams, impressions, situations, and prayers seemed to scream that he was 'the one'. In the end, the person all those things pointed to died and I was left with someone different—someone with whom I did not know how to connect. Something shifted in my heart that week, after one of our most robust disagreements about a contract of relationship expectations. As hard as I tried, I did not know how to connect with him anymore or how to lose my heart inside of his. For many years, I felt like we possessed one heart. That week, our heart started splitting. Eventually, it became two separate hearts and the one I was left with was broken. I came to realize emotional CPR was still necessary—but for me and my own heart. After losing such a large part of my heart, it was actually grief that taught me how to find it again.

December 2017

BROKEN HEART

As humans, we often feel a broken heart is the result of a lack of love. Yet, I wonder if part of the recipe for a broken heart is actually a broken capacity to love. A healthy heart can hold love—it sees broken love and acknowledges it for what it is, no more, no less. Likewise, it receives the full measure of healthy love—no more, no less. A broken heart, however, has a ravenous appetite for any kind of love, and from every type of love, it tries to indiscriminately extract more. Yet, more is never enough. Love will always fall through the cracks of a broken heart.

A healthy person will nourish herself. She will choose nutritious food, eat enough but not too much, put that food to good use—to exercise, to work. She is not afraid of junk food because she knows when to eat it, not to eat too much, and not to make it her sustenance. Quite the opposite, a person who is starving, who lives like an orphan or a poor man, is willing to eat anything. She will whittle garbage into dinner and never be full. So it is with love.

Tonight, my mother gently reminded me that being disappointed by love is part of living in a broken world. As humans, we carry this view that to be disappointed by love over and over, means there is something intrinsically wrong with us. It must mean we are unlovable. Maybe this sticks because there is a seed of truth to it, that I am just as broken as the person trying to love me. Maybe we do not receive love well when we have not yet learned the grace to love ourselves well. To love myself, I have to love all of myself; even the parts that are scary or unlovely. If I am running or hiding from these parts, pretending they do not exist—I do not have the capacity to receive love because I am not ready to say, "It is okay that you are broken. I am too. It is okay that you cannot fill me. I am already learning how to be full."

The thing is, Jesus Christ gave every person in the world permission to love him or herself because he gifted us with the opportunity to be free from our debts to shame. He gave us the affirmation that we all long for: the voice of someone better than ourselves telling us, "I love you just as you are." He came to prove the universe was conceived in love and is traveling toward a destiny of love; all of creation is a love letter. If we allow it, every piece of our lives can also become a part of this love letter.

I want to start stepping into this love letter by telling myself: it is okay to be broken. There is tenderness in it. It is okay to give grace for another's brokenness, even when it hurts me, because I am never without extravagant love. Mostly, it is okay to love in big, deep ways when it is unseen, unreturned, and not understood. It is okay because it is an act of agreement with the reality of unconditional love that I live in. In this reality, it is okay to fail. I am still figuring this out: how and why failure is okay, and how to get back up from it in grace and glory.

Maybe it is okay to fail because I was not made to be perfect. I was made to be loved and made perfect by love. Maybe it is okay to fail because it is an invitation for love to come a little closer and a little deeper. I think the reason failure is so terrifying is that people do not always love us through our failures. To love, knowing I will be rejected sometimes and loving anyway, sounds noble but makes me feel a little funny, a little naked, a little awkward. This process reminds me of words from an old hymn that Kyle and I used to sing when we first met, "Bind my wandering heart to Thee. "[1] Maybe part of what these words are saying is that God, who is love, is our calibration point. When I

---

1   Robinson Robert. "Come Thou Fount of Every Blessing." 1757.

fall down and face obstacles or pushback, I align with love, with the heart of God—not the response of another human.

In light of this, I want to say to the love that is coming, "I am sorry. I am sorry for depending on you to come and rescue me, to make me feel valuable. Jesus has already completed everything necessary to rescue me from shame, fear, self-loathing, and lovelessness. To expect this of you, my next love, is not living in the truth."

My mother likes to talk about the vows we make to ourselves as children, the unrealistic intentions for the future that we think will make our pasts okay. One vow I have held for a long time is that one day a man would love me. He would see me as beautiful, he would pick me and protect me. He would see worth in me that I could not see in myself and his loving me would prove to everyone who rejected me, overlooked me, and misused me, that I was worth something. I want to say to myself (and to God) that I am sorry. I am sorry for holding my worth to such a low standard, for living my life for people who never saw and probably never will see worth in me. I am sorry for believing another person held the key to my worth and that I needed a man in my life in order to love myself. I want to internalize the things I say I believe: that Jesus loves me. I do this by taking ownership of His gift of love and lavishing it on myself. When I cannot love myself, I want to rest in the assurance that He loves me still. I am still wholly loved, even when I fail myself.

I really do believe that a man will cherish me and pick me and, in some ways, protect me. Yet, I want to release expectations of him because love does not hold someone in a position of expectation. To the love that is coming after Kyle, whoever and wherever he is, I would like to say:

"Thank you for being you—the extraordinary and flawed you. I want to release you from an expectation to rescue a girl who has already been rescued by God. I want to release you from an obligation to make my heart okay, to respond to me in a certain way or time, because I do not want to come to you with a broken heart that will suck you dry. I want to come with a heart that has the capacity to love—to savor every piece of your love for what it is and release it for what it is not. I want to come to you with a capacity to love you—to make you feel seen, precious, and worthy, building you up and calling out life in you. I want to love you in all your inadequacies."

As I write this, the phrase that keeps coming to mind is "Love covers a multitude of sins."[2] We hate that word 'sin' in our culture, because misguided religion has often made it into a declaration of hopelessness, rejection, and condemnation. In actuality, sin is an archery term that means 'to miss the mark'.[3] It is

2   1 Peter 4:8 New International Version
3   Strong's Greek: 266. ἁμαρτία (hamartia) -—a sin, failure. (n.d.). Retrieved from https://biblehub.com/greek/266.htm

the word for all the things we do not like about ourselves—the habits we hate but keep returning to, all the times we fall short of who we want to be, all the ways in which we keep trying and trying and missing our target. It is a declaration of what we all know: we are all imperfect. A fundamental teaching of the Bible is that God loves you with all of your imperfections; His love is enough to meet you where you are and too great to let you stay as it found you.

So, to the love coming next: I want to make a patchwork love with you, to take my scrappy love and your scrappy love, putting them together like quilt squares, to make something beautiful that covers and protects. It will not be perfect, but Jesus can and will fill the holes. This is my promise to you, the love coming next: I will not hide. I will keep showing up, keep loving big, and keep pouring big cups of love on others, even when it is unseen, unreciprocated, or unrecognized. I will not waste it unwisely or dangerously, nor will I hold back in fear. And eventually, I will find you.

STILLNESS

When I think of the first Christmas following my breakup with Kyle, I think of stars: spots of radiance cutting through the darkness. When I visit my parents' home, I sleep in the attic. It is a large, spacious room with wooden floors and peaked ceilings. The iron bed I sleep in sits beneath a window with wooden shutters. Over the years, I would open these shutters on nights that I could not sleep. I would place my pillow at the foot of the bed, looking at the stars and think of God's famous words from the scriptures, "number the stars if you are able to number them,"[1] words that were given to illustrate a boundless promise. This practice has always reminded me of the possibility and adventure in a life with God, a life as limitless as the sky and studded with promises as abundant as stars.

Somehow, this process always made me feel more connected to Kyle. Maybe it was because in the very early days of our relationship one of the first things we did together was go to a star show. We sat on the floor of the forest and I threw my head back in wonder, looking

---

1   Genesis 15:5 English Standard Version

at the ceiling above us that was the sky. Shy and sweet, like all things in new relationships are, Kyle slipped his hand under my head and held it up the entire duration of the show so I could watch the stars in the comfort of his embrace without hurting my neck.

Over the years, no matter where we were in our relationship, no matter how far he was physically, emotionally, or relationally; looking at stars made me feel like we were still being held in the same canvas of endless possibility. There were so many sleepless nights I spent in that bedroom of my parents' house. There were nights when I longed for Kyle because we were broken up, nights when I did not know what would happen between us, nights when I was hurt by him, nights when I prayed for him, nights when I missed him, and nights when I wondered if he was missing me and praying about me too.

I laid under those windows, looking at those stars, one of the first times I decided to commit to a relationship with him—to really commit. I laid in that bed, under those stars, one of the first times I thought he broke my heart for good. I laid in the dark and sobbed and tried to imagine my life without him. There was comfort in the promise of possibility those stars spoke of. There always lingered the chance of a happy ending to all of this for us. I believed in that for so long—that we would eventually be married; and when we would visit my family at the holidays, Kyle would be there in that bed with me, and we would be gazing at the evening sky together. I would tell him of the times I prayed for him and thought of him, under those stars. The Christmas following our breakup, it was of course only me, surveying my life under those twinkling lights. I only ever laid alone under them, but this time there was a finality to it. It felt empty and hollow, but also thick with an assurance that things were as they should be.

With that recognition, I experienced grief over my life feeling stuck, different, and slower than I had imagined. Things felt like a dark night sky lasting longer than you expected it to. Cutting through this sadness with radiance, was the wonderfully mysterious pull of an unknown future. I could feel it and sense it, creating pockets of intoxicating beauty in my world. In the tension between the grief of the past and the promise for the future, I was consumed with an anxious energy. My heart was moving so quickly into a new season that I was unsure if my emotions would be able to keep up. I felt desperately excited for a new year, but also grippingly nervous for the unknown of entering the new year without Kyle.

My first Christmas without Kyle was special because, under the twinkling light of the stars, and the twinkling lights of the tree, I learned to feel the opposing emotions of grief and promise, anticipation and stillness. Before, they had felt disjointed, pushing and pulling my heart in a chaotic polarity. Yet, in the light of peace that only Christmas brings, they reached across my heart and held hands, tying together the past and the future, like a bow on a package, into a beautiful present.

December 2018

PRESENT

Christmastime is evocative. It is anticipatory, celebratory, and fabulously expressive to the point of frenzy. It is peaceful, white, and still in a way that arrests the world and grips the soul. In the middle of these twin natures, lies the holiday itself—Christmas Day.

To me, there has always been a tenderness in the dual natures of Christmas. It carries with it a brilliant hope that anything is possible, while illuminating all the bruises of disappointment from hopes that went another year unrealized and broken. It seems lately, my heart has been mirroring the pattern of the season and feeling the tenderness it brings.

Yesterday my friend Song shared this verse from the Bible. "Every good and perfect gift is from above, coming down from the Father of Heavenly lights, who does not change like shifting shadows."[2] With it, she wrote these words thick with anticipation and hope—"Good news is coming. The promises of God will become more visible, and things will surface now. Those who are hard hearted will become softened in their hearts. I see a horizon; I see the sun rising up like the morning dawn. I see rainbows from afar. I hear birds singing with expectations of what will come. Expect good things to come to you." After I

---

2   James 1:17 New International Version

read those words, I asked God about the new things unfolding in my life. "What will they look like?" I wondered. In response, I felt like I heard God say, "Wait until the new year and see what breaks on the horizon."

If the new year is my horizon and has a new future for me just around its corner, I feel like a child awaiting Christmas morning. The excitement is palpable, the joy is life giving, and the anticipation is almost unbearable. I know there are presents awaiting me, good things to unwrap as I unfurl myself into the morning of my new life. Yet not knowing what these gifts are exactly, I am filled with nervous anticipation. There is an element of agitation to my joy and excitement—a desire to rush through the present moment.

In stark contrast to this, I have felt an increasing pull to stillness all week long. There is a choir song we used to sing as children that has been playing in my head. I hear the words as I drive home, while I cook dinner, and while I brush my teeth. I hear the glassy voices singing about a stillness that is so intense, falling snow can be heard. The words "Fix your eyes on Jesus" have confronted me everywhere I turn this week as well, a whisper beneath the anxiety of my life, calling my heart to pause and focus.

Between packing for trips, planning for the holiday, and finishing exams, I have not quite known how to be still. All the frenzy has been conveniently fed by this pushing, driving anxiety in my heart. With

Christmas, there is excitement and introspection, celebration and stillness. Somehow, Christmas itself simply exists between the pull of these things. It is full of life and presence between the impossibly still and uncontainably expressive.

Today, I boarded a plane to head home for the holidays and for once, everything was incredibly quiet. There was no exam to prepare for, no class material to work through, and no medical journal article to read. It was just me, surrounded by strangers, earbuds in, with the monotonous hum of the aircraft in the background: a moment of presence between stillness and angst. In this moment, I discovered that there is another holiday existing between the call to peace and the impulse to anxiety. It is a state of simple existence in the presence of life's intensity: Sabbath.

Sabbath seems like such a word of antiquity, something crusty and irrelevant. Yet, the story of Christmas brings such deep beauty and significance to antiquity. The church understands Sabbath to be a day of rest or holiness, as is Christmas Day. I have been reading a book about Sabbath and today, as I flipped through its pages on my plane ride home, I read about it as something new. I read about Sabbath as a celebration: a time to celebrate the work that has been accomplished and the gifts that we already have, a day to trust that we are participants in God's work while acknowledging He is in control and in charge.[3]

---

3   Comer, J. M. (2015). Garden City: Work, Rest, and the Art of

With those words, I understood that excitement and stillness or celebration and sadness do not have to be polar. Sabbath is a holiday that unites these seemingly opposite emotions. On Sabbath, stillness *becomes* celebration. Gifts are found not by moving forward, though there is promise of goodness ahead, but by embracing the present moment, letting go of our need to advance our lives, and simply existing in joy.

The concept of Sabbath reminded me of the verse Song shared "Every good and perfect gift is from above, coming down from the *Father of Heavenly lights,* who does not change like shifting shadows."[4] I have been thinking all along that the good gifts will come with forward motion, through turning corners. Suddenly, I realize good gifts come from the light of God's presence. Sometimes the gift is the present. Sometimes the gift is the presence.

When I read these words about Sabbath, it felt like God breathed on them and I knew that between now and New Year, God was inviting me to a Sabbath. Sabbath is not only stillness or celebration; it is also surrender. One of the things I love most about Christmas Day is how the whole world stops. The streets are empty and the sky seems darker, lit only by the lights inside our houses, spilling their buttery hues through windows, like hundreds of

---

Being Human. Grand Rapids, MI: Zondervan.
4   James 1:17 New International Version. Emphasis Added

stars. All the shopping and gift wrapping, cooking and cleaning, music and festivities are preparation. They are the great crescendo preceding a moment of universal stillness. On Christmas Day, we stop and accept everything as it is—all that we have worked so hard to create, all that is left unfinished, all that we long for—and surrender them all to a moment of breathtaking wonder. Similarly in Sabbath, I sense an invitation to rest from the work of grief and surrender to life as it is in this moment. Beyond that, it is an invitation to step into a soft, clean, healing space with the "Father of Lights." It is creating space to let God fill my soul, to let Him seep in the way light seeps through windows and doors, brightening an entire room. It is a time to take a breath, releasing expectations, anxiety, and strategy for the future. A time to ask what God wants and how He wants to work, as I draw near to His heart. A time to listen in a way so still that I could hear the falling snow. In all the forward momentum, backward pull, and the exciting frenzy of my life, I feel God calling me to pause.

Where Sabbath leaves me is pausing in the middle—the uncomfortable place that is not exactly the exhilarating beginning and not exactly the resolving end. Today on the plane, I closed my book on Sabbath and turned on a podcast. The speaker started talking about the middle of things, how it is important to evade distractions and "fix our eyes on Jesus" in times like these. He reminded us that

Jesus starts and Jesus finishes. In the process: in the middle, in the waiting, wanting, and shifting, hearts are softened.[5] So, my call is to wait in the stillness of silence. I am still looking ahead toward my horizon but somehow, my eyes are fixed on Jesus.

Against the anxiety and rushing of my life, I am reminded of this phrase, "You can't force these things. They only come about through my (God's) Spirit."[6] Spirit—something so effortless and light, like tiny snowflakes that fall gently but change an entire scene. If I stop and take in this moment, I become aware of God reminding me that whatever is birthing itself in my life, whatever is rising on that horizon, is a work He started. He has a gift for me, and He wants me to give Him the room to unveil it to me, to surprise me with it in His own time.

When my plane touched down, I opened Instagram and saw a picture of a gorgeous snowy scene, capturing the essence of Christmas peace. The caption read, "At times, it is necessary to still our hearts before the Lord and let noise of all circumstances, relationships, and obligations fade away as we listen for His still small voice. It is in the stillness of heart that we are reminded of who we are and the majesty of God, His supreme authority, and His inexhaustible love for us. As we near Christmas

---

5   Veach, Chad, presenter. "Where Do You Turn in the Middle?" Zoe Church LA. 17 Dec. 2017. https://itunes.apple.com/us/podcast/zoe-church-la/id1071644334?mt=2
6   Zechariah 4:6 The Message

Day, let us draw near to His heart with intention, close enough to hear Him whisper. This year, we will give the greatest gift, our affection."[7] Right now, that feels comically ironic, because my bags were lost. As I write, I am stranded at the airport with nothing to do but to still my heart and reflect on God's words to me.

In response, I will gift God my heart. I will gift Him with all the love I have been trying to pin on the future. I will let Him pull me close. I will listen to the silence. As I do so, my heart feels soft and pure, as fresh as a white Christmas morning. It reminds me of these words "Blessed are the pure in heart, for they will see God."[8] I pray in this moment of Sabbath that God will keep me heart to heart with Himself. I pray that even as I hope for good gifts, He will help me truly release my expectations, not being focused on my own hopes or strategies for the future. I pray as I eliminate the distractions in this season, I would see God's face like never before. And now that I am finished writing, it would appear that my bags are here.

7   Circuit Riders, CRM Movement. Photo of House in Snow. Instagram, 22 Dec. 2017, https://www.instagram.com/crmovement/.
8   Matthew 5:8 New Living Translation

PART II
NEW BEGINNINGS

MORNING

The new year came with its promises of a new horizon. A few days into 2018, I found myself in Monterey. The following day was January 8, which reminded my soul of the number eight and how it represented a fresh start. It reminded me of all the significant eight's popping up in my life: of this new year 2018 and of the 5778 Jewish year I had been living in since September. The last time I had been in Monterey was with Kyle. We walked around the seaside town holding hands, looking at rings in boutique jewelry shops.

At first, being back in Monterey made me feel a little sad. In response, I kept telling myself, "It's okay. This is a new day to explore the better that is coming." Alongside that melancholy, I also held a quiet assurance that being in Monterey was a promise; Monterey is my city of new beginnings. It seems every time I am there, a significant new beginning is unfolding.

That day, as I watched deep blue water crash onto rocky cliffs, I reflected on the words that Song had written, for those of us in her prayer group, to read on the first of January.

"Happy New Year! Year 2018 will be ...

1. *A year of RESURRECTION. 2018 will be a year of "rising up" from our graves and walking out of our tomb. Your calling, your life, who you are, will be resurrected as you walk out of your tomb.*
2. *A year of a NEW ERA. Number 8 in the Bible represents Jesus, as in Greek, Jesus' name adds up to 888. It is also a number that signifies a new beginning, a new era. For those who followed Jesus with all their hearts, 2018 will be a year of a whole new beginning. God has started a new era for us, a new "age," a whole new season."*

These words reminded me of the building with the 888 address and the sign reading "new era, " I had seen on Rosh Hashanah and it seemed impossible that new life could be confirmed any more clearly to me. At the end of the day, I flew back to San Diego and as my plane took off, I felt in my heart that my life was taking off with it. These letters in Part II are the reflections from my emotional morning, in my first explorations of my new life.

GARDEN

$\mathscr{A}$ few years before Kyle and my's final attempt to make things work, we had gone through a heart wrenching preliminary breakup—giving each other up for, what we thought, was forever. This breakup was in fall. A few days after it, I read a love story that I had always carried close to my heart—a true love story, about a couple who knew they were meant for each other, yet also faced a season of having to give each other up, questioning everything. It had been instrumental in my initial decision to date Kyle and details of the story carried poignant similarities to details of our own relationship. Reading it again after this preliminary breakup, I came across a part of the story in which the main character receives an impression that his relationship, which was unraveling in autumn, would be resurrected in spring. I was unsure if those words were for me, but I counted the months until spring and realized they amounted to *seven* months. With that knowledge, I had a seed of hope for a spring resurrection. In the next seven months, it seemed that every scriptural metaphor of rain (which I associated with grief) developing spring resurrection, presented itself to me. These words especially rang true in this season, "Unless a grain of wheat is buried in the ground, dead to the world, it is never any more than a grain of wheat. But if it is buried, it sprouts and reproduces itself many times over."

Little did I know that, in the winter of our separation, Kyle was thinking and longing for me with such intensity, he said to God, "You have to bring me back this girl or take her off my mind." In response, he heard the simple heart impression, "It will be resolved in spring." At the time he prayed this, there was no communication between us but I had been praying for an early situational "spring." The simple reason for this was that February had always been a special month for Kyle and I. I wanted to observe all our treasured traditions and celebrations together, but spring does not come until after February. I prayed about this one night, as I got ready for bed. Between flosses and creams, the thought "Groundhog Day" shot into my head. I had heard of Groundhog Day but, living in California, I was more familiar with it as a funny Bill Murray movie than anything having to do with actual seasons. With a quick refresher on the holiday, I learned that it falls at the beginning of February and predicts whether an early spring will arrive. Little did I know that Kyle had also circled this day on his calendar. "Why do you care about Groundhog Day? Isn't that a holiday for second graders?," his co-worker had asked him. He chuckled, but miles away from me, he was also hoping for an early situational spring.

When Groundhog Day came, I found myself needing

to make an unforeseen trip to the grocery store. As I left the store that day, I paused, because next to the exit, stood a breathtaking array of colorful tulips. During college, when I lived in upstate New York, one of the first flowers to push through the ground after a snow, was the tulip. I pictured these bulbs bursting through the snow and thought to myself, "early spring." Almost simultaneously, I remembered that a few years before, I had written a love poem to Kyle about the dawning of spring after a rain of sorrow. One of the symbols I used, in the poem, to represent this spring was tulips—white and pure.

A few days later, I again needed to make a trip to the store. I decided as an act of faith for a new day, I would buy some tulips if they were in stock. They had to be white, like the tulips in the poem. When I arrived at the store, I walked all over the flower section and found tulips in every color but white. So, I called my mom and finished my grocery shopping, without tulips in hand. As I was about to leave, my mother began telling me about a dream she had. In the dream, God was bringing forth a harvest from things that had been damaged, transforming them into good seed. Exactly the moment when she told me that it was a season where God would bring forth good seed, I turned the corner and saw white tulips. When I took my little bundle of flowers home, my roommate mentioned that she loved them. I had kept my hopes for a rekindled romance a secret from everyone but one or two people in my life, and she was not one of them. Nevertheless, she glanced at them and said, "They're perfect for this season—they're like a fresh start."

That night, I broke the seven-month silence between me and Kyle with a text that read, "You are one of the most exquisite people I have ever met." We made arrangements to talk the next day. The following morning, I woke to these words, written by Song, who also had no idea what was going on with Kyle. They were written for a corporate group but addressed the exact passage of the Bible that I had been meditating on, regarding this situation.

"'After two days He (God) will revive us; on the third day He will restore us, that we may live in His presence. Let us acknowledge the Lord; let us press on to acknowledge Him. As surely as the sun rises, He will appear; He will come to us like the winter rains, like the spring rains that water the earth.'[1] *Spring is coming.* Something good will be released in the spring of this year. For those who have been in a *7-year* cycle, the Lord will bring a closure/conclusion to the final chapter of this cycle. I sense that God has been working in *7-year* cycles for some of you. To what God has started *7 years* before, He will bring a closure or conclusion that will be very evident to you. If you have been praying for *7 years* for something, you will see the result of your prayers. If you have been contending with an issue for *7 years*, God will give you a conclusion of some sort. If you have been in a *7-year* relationship with someone, something will shift

---

1   Hosea 6:2-3 New International Version. Emphasis Added

in the spring. I believe that we will experience a positive shift in the right direction. God will shine His light and fulfill the promises He made for us many years back. Have great hope! *Spring is coming!*"

I am not sure how to describe the exuberance I felt, marveling at how synchronously those words fit my situation—the confirmation of a promise for spring rebirth and the seven-year blessing I longed for. That day, Kyle and I entered into a relationship again. Seven months later, I said goodbye to him for the final time in the parking garage, finding myself disappointed, confused, heartbroken, and searching for spring in the ashes of my life.

In the November following our breakup, I received a book in the mail, called *Garden City*. It was white with the title written in big, *gold* letters across the cover. Little did I know that this book, which was not about grief at all, would somehow become a metaphor for the next season of my life. The season felt like a cyclical recurrence of the loss/hope/resurrection cycle I had endured with Kyle over and over through the course of our relationship. Yet, no matter how many times Kyle and I failed a spring rebirth, spring itself regenerated.

January 2018

GARDEN, CITY

This morning, I thought about a few lines from a Bible passage, "Wake up. Put your face in the sunlight. God's bright glory has risen for you....They'll confer a title on you: City of God."[2] These verses remind me that I want a heart like a city. I want a heart buzzing with light and life—a heart that is generative for the good of others. I want to be known as a city of God, a place where He loves to dwell. Yet, this is not what I see when I look at my life. My mother said that she can perceive my new season already sprouting up, but that I cannot yet distinguish the sprouts from the weeds. I feel this too but with a longing to see beyond sprouts.

Recently I read another piece of scripture and the language arrested me. "They will come and sing aloud *and* shout for joy on the height of Zion (a mountain), and will be radiant [with joy] over the goodness of the Lord... And their life will be like a watered garden and they shall never sorrow or languish again."[3] To never *languish* again, to shout with joy over the goodness that has happened in my life—that is what I want. Yet when I study these words, I see those things come from a garden place; I am reminded, at its core, my heart has always been a garden. My heart will always be an unseen place where beauty is grown, slowly, arduously, with great nurture.

The thing about a garden is that it is a hidden place of great vulnerability where patience is required. A city is a place of "right now". It is supersaturated with life, color, and noise. It is flashy

2   Isaiah 60:1b, 14a The Message
3   Jeremiah 31:12 Amplified Bible

and ostentatious. Nothing is hidden about a city. A garden is a place of wait and see. Life is fragile in the garden. No one sees the seeds underground and no one cares that they are there. Life arrives in ways that are miraculous but quiet and unnoticed. You never truly know if life will arrive at all or if it will languish under the weight of the seasons. The garden is where I find my heart.

Right now, there are things in my life for which I desire answers. I hold a vision for my life, and I want to know if I am moving towards it. Over the last few days, I have felt God saying that He is not going to give me the answers yet. In this place, I want to hide. I am still a little fragile from the past season and it is easier to have a yes or a no, than to open up my feelings to God. It is easier to ignore my hopes than to plant them and have them fail again. Yet I sense that in the unknown, God does not want me to hide the desires of my heart from Him. Rather, He longs for me to be vulnerable with Him. In trusting Him, I am letting Him back into my tender places; my garden places.

This morning, I woke up to words about waiting, in a blog a friend had written. She wrote how in seasons of waiting, God is actively at work in ways that are invisible to us. She used the example of planning her daughter's eighth birthday celebration; about all the work she did unbeknownst to her daughter, to make sure the perfect celebration was in place. She suggested that similarly God is working behind the scenes, "to launch you into your destiny." In this way, God is the Master Gardener. His Spirit is always moving over the seeds I plant, even when they are far beyond the reach of my hands.

The scripture passage that was on my heart this morning is from a book in the Bible called Isaiah. I have been thinking a lot about this book because it talks about destruction and rebuilding, loss and joy, gardens, and cities. The chapter I have most recently been reading ends with this verse—"For as the earth bursts with spring wildflowers, and as a garden cascades with blossoms, So the Master, God, brings righteousness into full bloom and puts praise on display before the nations."[4] Immediately, the next chapter begins by talking about a city. These words of transition tell about a planted garden breaking forth into a city, which further impressed on me that with God, gardens are inextricably connected to cities. I have all along been thinking that God loves to dwell in cities: in well cultivated places, where life abounds. I always saw cities as places of instantaneous growth. Yet, this verse causes me to think that God loves to dwell in gardens, cultivating cities from them. He loves to rest in the shade of our thoughts and the fragile flowers of our desires, artfully nurturing them until they bloom. It is from the secret and slow, silent and still, the unexpected and intimate, that God births vibrant vision and brilliant life. Public

---

4   Isaiah 61:11 The Message

flourishing comes from private growth. The garden grows into a city, becoming a garden city. It is both a place of tender nurture *and* generative creativity. As I again wait for spring rebirth, I will nurture small shifts, trusting they are sprouts that will grow into something glorious, public, and full of light, like a city.

HEART GROWING

With all the excitement I held for spring, February hit me like a tsunami mixed with a ton of bricks. I entered the month with high hopes, but what happened was like a Pinterest fail—the differences between my expectations and reality were painfully dissimilar. It was damp and rainy, and life felt heavy in general. I do not know if there was more water coming from the sky or my eyes. It was the month of so many shared traditions with Kyle: the month of the anniversary of our getting back together to get married, and of course the month of Valentine's Day. As much as I had been determined to stay hopeful and embrace the shift, I felt like I had been crushed. I was just trying to stay afloat and make it to March.

I usually love Valentine's Day and looked forward to this holiday to cheer me up. Usually, my mother and sisters mail me homemade cards, constructed with red paper, fancy scissors, and glitter. I hoped (more like desperately prayed) that someone in my life would send me flowers. When the day came, all but one sister had been too busy to make cards and because of the busyness, we barely talked over the phone. I was too inundated with school tasks to make anything chocolate and no one sent me flowers. On that day something snapped, and I again felt the weight of all I had walked through in the past year. For the rest of February, I allowed myself to grieve how different this month was from what it had been in the past and what I imagined it to be in the future. Although it felt like drowning, it was actually growing.

February 2018

LOVE MONTH

Yesterday was not the Valentine's Day I prayed for. It was emotional and exhausting. I wanted a day about the fluffy feelings of love and God ended up giving me a day that was about real love—about waiting, patience, unselfishness, and healing. I have been praying about how to make room in my heart for the love coming next. Yesterday, I was reminded to not make the next love about getting my needs met, but rather about loving another person unselfishly. I was also reminded that sometimes in faith we take action, but other times we wait.

Lately, life and grief have obscured any sprouts of the new season I thought I saw. Today, a new light washed over my feelings. I wondered if the new season is not as distant as it feels, but rather so close I do not even recognize it. Perhaps all this heartache which seems to be suffocating my future, is actually the foundation my life is expanding from.

This thought reminded me of a situation that happened to me recently, when I applied for a home service that would help me save money. After I applied, I thought I was rejected because I experienced a long period of hearing nothing. In the end, a processing mistake was made, and I was credited with free retrograde services in addition to what I had applied for. Maybe the same thing is happening in the silence of my heart, the silence of all I hope for in my future. It is carving out space for greater abundance than what I can now imagine.

I have been praying that, in my waiting, God will be expanding. On Valentine's Day, almost in response to my prayer, I stumbled across a poem. It was written beneath a photo of a couple nestled close in the snow, surrounded by softly glowing lights. The words beneath it talked about learning to become wholehearted before finding your next love, and that when you suck love into your brokenness, all it does is fill your holes. But when you add love to your wholeness, it grows and spreads. The poem talked about love that sets things ablaze and about illuminating cities. Reading it, I thought of the language of fire and cities God has been using to speak to me lately, and my heart felt warm. It felt like a light had been turned on inside me, like the ones in the photos, glowing bravely against the bleak world around it. I thought of the letter I wrote to the love coming next, about wanting to come wholehearted. I wondered if during this waiting, this pause, this space between the known and the unknown, the inhale and the exhale, God is answering my prayer. He is expanding my heart to receive what is coming in a way that will not leak and is not broken. God is teaching me a fullness independent of any love in the past and any love on its way. Maybe in a space that feels dark, God is transforming me into a heart that could set my garden city on fire.

ATTACHMENT

One of the most special experiences in my life occurred when Kyle and I found ourselves at a coffee shop, selecting a date for our wedding. It became special for an entirely different reason. We had kicked off the morning with some serious conversations and this unintentionally triggered new memories of childhood trauma I experienced. I saw myself in this trauma alone, remembering a piece I had never recalled before. The memory completely enveloped me, and I began convulsively sobbing in public. Over and over, I heard Kyle's voice saying, "Chelsea, look at me. Chelsea, look at me." I did not look at him. My eyes were directed downward, as I nearly hyperventilated, and his voice was like one on the other end of a muffled telephone. He persisted and gently guided my face so that my eyes could meet with his. "Chelsea, you're okay. Chelsea, you're okay." He spoke softly to me as if soothing a child. Suddenly, for the first time in my life, someone had physically inhabited a situation with me in which I had previously felt totally alone. And it was not just someone. It was the person I loved with all my heart. He pulled me to his chest and cried over me, then prayed over me. He prayed for me that I would know that I am clean. I do not know if I ever felt more like I belonged to him than in that moment.

This story reminds me of why I loved Kyle. It also reminds me of how tears, like rain, are cleansing. I cannot deny knowing Kyle was cleansing. First, the love I carried for him cleansed me. Then, the grief I carried for him cleansed me. In the same way, there is something about revisiting attachment, about feeling forbidden and forgotten emotions that moves you.

The night I transcribed this letter, I discovered that exactly one year since the first day after our discussed wedding date, Kyle was no longer connected to me in a way he used to be. I was surprised to find some residual grief in this. I had disconnected from him, in this capacity, a year ago. Even so, *his* decision to disconnect added a finality to the death of his love for me, to the uncrossable chasm that had grown between us—a chasm created by choice. He was really gone. With that realization, this was the perfect letter to transcribe that night. It is one of my favorites because I read it aloud to Sarah, who first presented me with the challenge of writing it. Of all the letters I read to her, I remember the way my heart split, as I read this one. I remember how I cried more heavily in reading this letter than perhaps, in reading any other letter. Yet my tears were to my heart, as a river to a rock— splitting, softening, reshaping. As the tears rolled down my face, I allowed Kyle to roll off my heart in new ways. Tonight, I cannot think of a better thing to do than appreciate the beauty of attachment—sometimes attachment moves us towards others, but sometimes it moves us forward from them. I have learned that no matter which direction attachment moves us, like tears or rain, it cleanses our hearts and reveals to us the first day of a new life.

February 2018

DEAR "ATTACHMENT,"

The first words that came to my mind when challenged by Sarah to write a letter to "attachment", were "dear darling." I thought this was strange for something impersonal that I am trying to let go of. Yet, when I think of my attachment to Kyle, I think of a part of me that feels alive—this happy, sunny person, who is seen, known, loved, and has value. It is a piece of myself that I have not felt since before I began grade school.

I remember the trepidation I felt entering kindergarten. It is ironic that I felt this way. I was bright and effervescent; I loved people. Yet for some reason, I possessed a fear of being left behind by the rest of the kids. School brought a lot of hardships. The kids were wealthy and cliquey, and it felt like I never got picked for anything. When I was five or six years old I was molested (more than once) by the husband of someone at the school. At such a young age, this was the one thing I felt "picked" for, a feeling as confusing as it was awful. I carried this wound with me from that day forward—the feeling of being less than other girls; a wound amplified by the fact I was continually ostracized and never the favorite. I stayed with the same group of kids from elementary school until high school. There were periods when the rejection was not so bad and we all played together as kids should, but I always felt like I was the odd man out—a little awkward, somewhat under-talented, not pretty or likable, unable to break into social groups. In high school, everything exploded into one big, backstabbing mess involving mean, exclusive, threatening behaviors that made me feel isolated. I lost all of my lifelong "friends." Nobody showed up for me or showed loyalty to me, not even the ones I loved and cared about. I became extremely sick, left school, and watched as my life took another path.

Then, I met Kyle and he lit me up inside. He made me feel seen, cherished, valued, loved, and known, like nobody ever had before. He was this dynamic force that curled up inside my soul and wanted to stay forever! Even more amazing, I loved him back. It was like I had known him and waited for him all my life and he felt the same way about me. We could spend hours talking and connecting; just being together was magic. Shortly after he met me, Kyle sent me the lyrics of a song called *First Day of My Life* and we used to write the lyrics back and forth to each other over the years. It is a song about a man learning to love a woman and how that love changes him. The singer talks about how the very sight of the woman he loves causes him to be reborn into a whole new world he did not know existed. He experiences seeing her face as if being healed from blindness, and walks out into a day full of rain, watching it transform into a day full of sun. At the end of these realizations, he finds himself in that raw place we all find ourselves after encountering earth shaking love. He is not quite sure where he is or where he has been before, but he knows he wants his path to move toward this love. Although his process is slow, he realizes his need for this woman, which points him to her, to home.

I still feel deeply when I hear this song; it reminds of how Kyle and I felt about each other. Today, it rained hard. The morning after Kyle and I broke up it rained, even though it was August. I kept thinking about how cleansing rain is. Classes started again today and one of my teachers mentioned how some cultures believe it is good luck when it rains on the first day you start something. As it rained, that song, *First Day of My Life*, which I have not thought of in a while, began playing in my head. I remembered specifically the part that talks about life starting over when the singer walked out into the rain.

As I reflect on attachment, I realize how Kyle made me feel alive for a little while. Yet recently, for the first time since going to primary school, I have had these breakthrough moments of feeling alive—of feeling exuberant joy for no other reason than gratitude over the wonder and beauty of life.

Moments of feeling brave and free, like I can breathe for the first time in a long time. It feels like the first day of my life, in a totally new and unexplored way. It is like grieving Kyle has been the doorway allowing me to access the grief I have carried all my life. For the first time, I am grieving—I feel all the rejection, sadness, and broken pieces I could never bring myself to feel, wringing themselves out of my soul.

If there is more to my grief over Kyle, I wonder if there is also more to my attachment to Kyle. Today, I thought about the part of the song that compares loving someone to going home and I wondered if there were unrealized patterns in my dynamic with Kyle that felt a little too much like something I already knew. Was I attached to the fear that the best version of love I could get was a cleaned up version of the "acceptance" I learned as a child? An acceptance that came through making all that I am, disposable to a man's pleasure. Was some of the attachment I felt to Kyle a "going home" in a way, an attempt to recreate the broken dynamics of love and acceptance I felt as a child, but in a little less broken way?

Beyond subliminal patterns, there is real love involved in my attachment to Kyle. I would be dishonest if I did not recognize that Kyle loved me the most real way he knew how. I feel like this year is going to be my best year yet, like I am going to the most exuberant and exciting places in my life thus far. And Kyle, this person who was my heart for seven years, cannot come. It feels like leaving "home" behind. Nothing made this reality more poignant than something that happened over the holidays.

I traveled to one of my favorite places with my sister. The problem was, it was also a favorite spot shared by Kyle and I. On the trip with my sister, I brought along all the accouterments Kyle and I had purchased for visits there together— accessories for a trip we never took. I had been okay visiting this place without him, up to that point. This time, however, my cousin (who first introduced us) was staying at Kyle's house and I was not. My cousin joined Kyle's family Christmas list and I did not. My cousin wanted to get together to see us, and as far as I could tell, Kyle did not. Suddenly, I was no longer invited to the place that was supposed to be our shared home. I had to drive by it multiple times on my way to and from our destination, and again to meet my cousin at the little cafe near Kyle's house. That cafe was where he and I first planned our logistical steps to spending our lives together, over cups of steaming hot coffee and tea. It was the spot where we often spent sunny mornings brunching. Kyle did not acknowledge I was in town or say we were welcome to see my cousin at his house. Maybe he did this out of respect for me, but in it, I felt him detaching from me in a way he never had before.

It has been over three months since I told him I wanted a three-month break from talking and I have not heard from him, which is unprecedented for our relationship history. Something inside me feels like he does not want or long for me the same way he used to. I think he still loves and maybe even misses me, but something is different. All of this has carried some grief for me. Most painful is the realization that we do not have "home" together anymore. His home is not a place I can call home, and his heart is not a place I can go home to.

When I was with my cousin, he mentioned how he slept in Kyle's bed, while Kyle slept on the couch. I thought of all the women who might have slept in Kyle's bed since we broke up, and it stirred up this familiar sadness in me. It was the sense of rejection, love lost, and realization that even though I freely gave my heart to Kyle, I did not feel like he gave his heart as freely to me. I again felt how deeply I wanted to mean something to him.

From the day I met him, I possessed a deep resolve not to be a girl he dated without meaning, and as I grew to love him, I desperately wanted to touch and hold his heart. While he loved me in a way he loved no one else, I feel like my desire never truly came to pass. Whenever we broke up, there were dozens of other women that he would easily jump into planning a life with. Or more accurately, jump into bed with. I felt like his attachments to these women overshadowed me and took away from the sacredness of the spot I held in his heart. They kept me from really possessing his heart and prevented him from giving me the dignity of grieving, of feeling the emptiness of losing me as I felt for him. Sometimes holding onto attachment is easier than acknowledging how someone I loved with my whole heart did not love me back in the way I wanted—nor did he grieve me in the way that I wanted, and there is nothing I can do to earn his love or remorse.

Attachment to Kyle has also perpetuated a sense of obligation. I want him to experience real love so badly. I think of all the ways that I knew him, saw him, and loved him. I think of all the things we experienced together and all the times he told me I was the only woman he ever *really* loved. I fear if I am not with Kyle, he will not experience real love. I fear he will settle. The truth is, I could be with Kyle and that does not mean he would experience real love. I cannot force on him what he does not want. Right now, he does not want real love. If he did, he would have been willing to be there for me when I needed him, to love and support the person I am and not just the fantasy he wanted me to be.

When I was a child, I found a crappy substitute for love and through a lot of rejection, came to believe that sacrificing myself to others' demands was a necessary prerequisite for acceptance; some love is better than none. Maybe my attachment to Kyle has soothed the fears related to this. Yet I feel that in this freedom I have experienced since breaking up, a bold declaration is happening in my life. It is a declaration that I refuse to settle for this old model of love. I refuse to believe that the only way I can be cherished and known is by giving up myself for someone else's pleasure. I am learning to live in this truth by learning to have a healthy heart. I have to realize that I have outgrown one type of love, and more courageously, have to believe there is another kind of love I am ready for, and it will pick me back. So even though it stings a little, I am learning to be okay with Kyle moving on. And in releasing him over and over again, I am discovering the first day of a new life.

HEART TIRED

When I dated Kyle, one of the softest things in the world to me was trying to coordinate our breath. We would lay sideways on the bed or the floor, the sides of our bodies gently touching. We would close our eyes, place our heads near each other, and breathe. Inhale, exhale—trying to do it at the exact same time. I loved the way this lit up the moment. I could feel the way his breath created a gentle rise and fall of his skin—a tiny detail about him I would never notice in an ordinary moment. I loved the way I could feel his heartbeat—wildly, erratically beating through his chest and pulsing through his arms. "Your heart is beating so fast," I whispered once. "I'm nervous," he whispered back, blushing softly. There was something about this practice that created such a state of existence—so easy, so soft, so natural. When we were there, we were so connected to each other and everything around us. It felt like we were holding each other's hearts.

That is something I had to relearn as I unfolded into the new year following our breakup. I had to learn to wake up from the exhaustion of my grief and breathe—to be and exist in the world around me in a way that was soft, easy, and natural. The key to that, I learned, was vulnerability—which was anything but soft, easy, and natural. In the first few months of the new year, this phrase kept rolling around in my head: "Courage: in the new season, I have to say things I wouldn't normally say and do things I wouldn't normally do." I made vulnerability my hobby and I did just that. I practiced kindness for no other reason than being kind. I encouraged strangers, showed up to be seen, and probably overshared a little. My process was messy, but bold and sincere. Each act was a streak of paint on the canvas of my new life. Somehow, though the colors bled and dripped, they ran together, making something beautiful. And it felt awful, like being punched in the gut. I felt naked and exposed— like someone was going to call me out as a fraud at any moment. In all my running, painting, and being kind, I had forgotten to hold my own heart. I have come to believe this is one of the ways we cover the nakedness of vulnerability. We inhabit our breath, holding space with our own hearts.

February 2018

BREATHING

A few weeks ago, I read these stunning words by one of my favorite poets:

"Slow down. Breathe with me. Breathe *with* me. The quiet between us today is one full of longing, of hope, albeit, a tired one.

But, here, for the time being, I can't help but think
'you know, maybe it's okay to be tired.'
I do believe we can make it.
I do believe I'll find my words again and that
goodness is just around the corner, even listening
closely with a sweet smile.
I'm not lost, just somewhere new.
I'm just somewhere that's still expanding beneath
me
And though it might take some practice to balance,
I don't imagine it will be long before these dim,
narrow passes open right up to broad and open
fields—a world dancing lovely with a gentle breeze.
So let us lay here and breathe
It's to remind my weary, tender heart
that fresh air is out there and it's not all that far off
now."[1]

After reading this, I happened upon a handful
of other poems about breath, how it simultaneously
cleanses and pulls us into ease, and how the dearest
and truest friends sit with you in that space of
nothing more than breathing. Along with these
thoughts, I remembered a favorite song about how
God Himself supports our breath. Not only does He
support it, He, Himself is in our breath. According
to scholars, the name used for God in the Hebrew

[1]   t.r.h.   blue From "We're Just Somewhere New" www.
notesontheway.com. Used with permission.

scriptures is beyond pronunciation, able only to be experienced as breath. There is something very sacred about the Creator of the universe desiring Himself to be experienced as something as simple and powerful as an inhale and exhale. Both God and breath are invisible. In breath, God reminds us that He inhabits every moment, that the infinite is somehow contained in the intimate. With His very essence, He is teaching us how to breathe when we do not yet know the outcome and it feels like the world will fall apart if we fall into something as easy as breathing. In the moments when all we can feel are the chaos, uncertainty, and heaviness of life, He seeps under the heaviness like vapor or mist, curling Himself under our flesh, next to our hearts, sustaining the rhythm of life itself: the up and down, in and out, rise and fall, ebb and flow. He is not only there in those moments, but as the song reminded, the moment between the two—the middle.

In my life right now, I breathe deeply, feeling tired and strong at the same time. One of the reasons I stayed for so long with Kyle is because I believed God had good plans for us to be together. There was one experience of wonder after another, indicating to me that God was in this, His favor was with me, and He had good plans for Kyle and I. I was careful at first, to believe that God was in my desire to be with Kyle, because I try to listen for what God is actually saying, instead of trying to spiritualize what I want Him to say. What I want

Him to say is not always perfect and good. In my relationship with Kyle, I filled two journals recording the amazing signs that pointed toward relationship with him, and I continuously sought outside advice from wiser people, to check my thought process. In our relationship, I fought not only for what I loved, but also for what I believed in, until I was released. At the end of our relationship, when the way we had worked our unhealthiness into unsolvable tangles was unbearable, I knew my time with Kyle had expired and I felt a weight being lifted.

I do believe that in the course of our relationship, God stepped into my desire to be with Kyle and used it as a divine invitation to him: an invitation to step into something good and pure that God had in store for us. When Kyle chose not to step into a relationship with me in the capacity that I knew was best for my soul, I felt like God said to me, "Time to go" for my own good. Yet, I had risked feeling crazy and being wrong to cast a bet on the side of hope. I fought hard and did not get the outcome I wanted. I am okay with that now, because I have space for something better. Yet, the process of carving out that space was exhausting.

I came out of this season with a lot of doubt. I experienced months of intense anxiety, with Kyle's questions about our differing beliefs running through my head—sifting through history, archeology, geology, philosophy, thinking in circles, afraid of this question: was everything I have built my life on a delusion? If it was, what is truth? I never ended up solving all the mysteries of science and history. Nevertheless, I am learning to be okay with uncertainty because I arrived at this realization: our knowledge and discovery is incredible, providing tools to guide our understanding of the world around us. In the same breath, they are also just a snapshot in time. I reflect on all of the thinkers of centuries past, how they were exceedingly talented, but had incomplete knowledge. What made perfect sense 1,000 years ago is laughable now. That is the human condition and so, I think the foundation of my life has to be something more transcendent than knowledge—something like love, truth, humility, grace, forgiveness, and peace. Something that has never changed and never will, must come from somewhere.

There is a story in the Bible, about a man who hears God's voice. He goes from a season of intense loneliness to essentially the pinnacle of his "career" in a matter of days. His mountaintop moment is characterized by some pretty miraculous events, but also intense fighting for what was right. The day following this climax, he receives death threats and runs away into the wilderness by himself. He despairs that he failed, and asks God to die. In response, an angel is sent to him that basically tells him to sleep and eat.[2]

---

2   1 Kings 18-19

Although Song does not know much of my backstory with Kyle, she messaged me to tell me she felt like I was similar to this man in the Bible. She wrote, "While you may feel like you've been battling all alone, I hear the Lord saying He is with you and you will see miracles this year." In this story, the man of God was victorious, but he did not feel like it. He felt defeated and tired, physically and emotionally. It reminds me of how I feel right now.

So during this time, I am pausing and breathing—learning it is okay to be tired and that breathing feels a lot like vulnerability. Both are this soft state of being and existing, when everything else is stripped away. They are stillness and movement at the same time. Both require you to inhabit the sacred space between the inhale and the exhale, the beginning and the end, the known and the unknown. That is where I am living right now. It is both terrifying and exciting.

The terror I seem to be wrestling with the most right now, is worthiness. How do I engage the world from a place of worthiness? I am a little clunky at that right now. Nevertheless, it is key to keep trying, because cultivating worthiness invites what will unfold in the exhale. This is a hard concept for me. I started this letter, wrote up to this point, and left it unfinished for at least three weeks. To begin unraveling this subject from my heart, I must acknowledge how I never felt worthy of Kyle, or with Kyle. I felt like I did not live up to his past girlfriends—not smart enough, pretty enough, soft enough, sexy enough, to live up to these women who, in my mind, were still his girlfriends. I feel unworthy of being a wife and mother, of experiencing sex where I am cherished and valued. Although I know my beliefs about my worth are untrue, there is a piece of me that feels like I am without these things because I am unworthy of them, even worse—like I have failed in them. To further complicate the matter, I feel like I failed *because* I am intrinsically unworthy of the things I desire and if I was not so broken in these areas, I would have already been picked for them.

In this place of preparing for the new, I have felt unworthy of the type of partner and people I would want to pick me. I think I have a lot to offer. Still, it feels like everything I have, someone else has better or more of. Whenever I take small steps toward connection, I think of all the reasons someone should reject me, and I am left wondering: why would anyone pick me? I want to shift this question to: why *wouldn't* someone pick me?

I want to learn to breathe: to inhabit and hold my own space. I am learning there are people in this world worthy of my wholeheartedness—people who I want to show up for, who I want to take the risk of being seen for—people who are worthy of the love and attention I can give when I live from a place of worthiness. To believe others do not want me because I am flawed, is to ironically rob others of my best self.

Living out the belief I am worthy requires vulnerability. Vulnerability requires having the courage to show up and be seen. I have been thinking about all the ways I am showing up and being seen in my life. I am going to church without lumping the beautiful people there into the same box as the church people I knew in the past and forgiving both when they bear similarities. I am sharing more of the thoughts that come out of my journey, reaching out to people and making new friends. I am using the names of new friends instead of saying "that guy" or "this person" as a safeguard, in case we do not stay friends. I am asking questions instead of shutting a conversation down so I do not have to risk being shut down myself. I feel exposed, but brave.

In this process, I am reminded of Jesus' words, "Come to me, all you who are weary and burdened, and I will give you rest. Take my yoke upon you and learn from me, for I am gentle and humble in heart and you will find rest for your souls.[3]" Jesus meant it. He was the most humble person in history. He grew up in a nowhere town, in an insignificant and oppressed nation. Not even in His hometown was He wanted, because of His lacking pedigree. Even so, Jesus revolutionized history: always full of civic respect, trying to keep His works personal and unadvertised, never self-promoting. In the end

---

3   Matthew 11:28-29 New International Version

the books written about Him outnumber any other historical manuscript. Jesus spent time with people we would view as unworthy—simple, uncomfortable, unwanted people, and He loved them. People like me. I am learning to follow suit, spending time with and learning to love myself.

I am starting with these affirmations, which I wrote to myself during a particularly scary moment of vulnerability—words of love to myself:

"I am proud of you
I am proud of you for letting yourself be seen
I am proud of you for reaching out
I am proud of you for taking risk
I am proud of you for offering your heart

I would do it again
I would do it again if you are turned down
I would do it again if you are never
acknowledged
I would do it again if all goes well

I will hope for success with you
I will embrace failure with you
BE UNAPOLOGETICALLY YOU

I will release expectations with you
I will release expectations of others to
respond to your love with a certain outcome, in a
certain way, or certain time

Because that is what love does.

I will love you just as you are
I will settle with you into the home for your heart
that is here and now, that already exists
I will give kindness, whether it is received or not
I will give kindness, whether it is recognized or not
I will give kindness, whether it is understood or not
I will do this with joy
Because your life is radiant glory to God in the
Highest.
God sees unseen kindness—to Him it is art, to me,
a gift"

When I think about breathing, about Jesus' words inviting rest, I feel like God is telling me that I do not have to white knuckle worthiness—some days I do not feel like speaking those declarations over myself and that is okay, because when I do not, He will. He will keep at it until I believe them too. Just breathe. Just show up. Be brave, even if that is just breathing and bringing your best. He is here, in this moment, in the middle, in the vulnerability, and in every breath.

BABIES

A few weekends ago, I spent some time with a couple of friends in their old, craftsman style house in Los Angeles. The husband of this couple is one of my oldest friends, and his wife is a wonderful woman who I watched him learn to love over the past eight years. This year, they had a baby, and witnessing my friends transform into a mother and a father before my eyes reminded me of the wonderful way love weaves itself around us.

There is something miraculous in the way babies change our concept of time. The weekend of my visit we spent Saturday afternoon listening to records, nibbling cheese and scones in the sunshine, and marveling for hours over the faces made by their little, blue-eyed miracle. We were happy like that. There is something about a baby that stretches moments of wonder into hours, and hours into years, then into a lifetime. A baby is this little seed of possibility, with so much hope and unknown in one small bundle of flesh. With a baby, the smallest thing takes up the most room in the heart. It is for all these wonderful, mysterious reasons that I think looking into the eyes of a baby can feel like holy ground.

There is something about grief that feels like that too. It slows down moments, creating a holy ground of its own. This holy ground is the middle—that space occurring after the sadness lifts, the anger dissipates, and the loneliness lessens, where you begin to dream a little. You allow yourself to hope for new happiness. However, it feels slightly less miraculous and exponentially more awful, than looking into the eyes of a baby. The essence of hope demands existence in a vulnerable place, in which the outcome of that hope, the tangibility of the new life, is wildly uncertain.

My friends' baby is named Blythe. This name is derived from a word that means "to be joyfully unconcerned and unworried"—a word that embodies aliveness. Blythe reminds me of what hope in the vulnerable place feels like. It feels like the whole world is encompassed in one very fragile seed that is immeasurably precious to your heart. It feels like something ever so tiny that overcomes all of your other emotions. It feels like an excitement for possibility that cannot be contained, even while you do not know if it will actually come to pass. It feels like this wild thing, wriggling between the hands you try to grasp it with, stretching moments into hours, feelings into seasons, and vulnerability into a destination of its own. It feels like daring joy in the face of uncertainty, the bravery to be unworried about the unknown, and the holy first step to re-inhabiting your heart as fully alive.

February 2018
HOPE

Last night, as I was falling asleep, this phrase rolled into my head: *Waiting is creating space for expectation to grow. Like being pregnant, waiting is holding space to nurture expectation without yet delivering it.*

Today I woke up and listened to a message from my old church. The speaker talked about waiting and he likened it to pregnancy. He mentioned how when couples get pregnant, they wait to tell people until a certain point in the pregnancy, because there is a vulnerability in not knowing what will happen. Similarly, he likened things we hope for to this pregnancy pattern. There are things in life for which we can identify the outcome we desire, but remain uncertain as to how they will actually be delivered. He pointed out how sometimes, we hold these things close to our hearts and do not announce them, because we are afraid to get our hopes up. Yet, he mandated that we do just that! While listening, I was reminded of a song I found the morning after Kyle and I broke up. It is called *Get Your Hopes Up*, which did not make any sense at the time. Yet, I knew it would be one of the soundtracks of my new life.

As I listened to this message, I wondered if there is a piece of me that is holding back from the goodness of the new season, because I feel afraid. With Kyle, I feel like I gave birth to a stillborn promise. I deeply felt the pain, love, and emotion involved in bearing and losing that promise. I do believe God has promised me a full-term "baby" of promise but I am afraid to hope because it feels risky and vulnerable. In the light of all the hopes for Kyle that crumbled into bitter disappointment, I wonder how much I can trust my own hopes.

This reminds me of my letter to the garden places of my heart and God's challenge to trust Him with my unknowns. It is funny to think you could be vulnerable with someone who knows you better than you know yourself. I am realizing that God's desire for my vulnerability is not about Him gaining knowledge. It is about my offering to Him, the places I am afraid of letting someone else hold. Instead of offering them, I have been holding back. I have been holding my hopes close because I am afraid of feeling like a foolish girl who let my heart run away. It seems impossible for life to go the direction I hope. Yet, even more than I am afraid, I want to take ownership of my ideas and believe that they are possible. I am going to take risks in my life. My question is: How do I overcome the paralysis of fear to walk in bravery? When I asked God "How do I become brave?" I heard in response, "*LOVE* MAKES YOU BRAVE."

I am learning a bravery developed through fire: the strength and resiliency formed when love goes through hate and comes out the other side still love. I hear God asking me to keep my heart open to Him, others, and life itself when all my heart wants to do is involute itself. Bravery feels a little unsafe because love is what tore me apart in the past season. It would be easier to stay in a place of anger or guardedness but love holds the key to the next chapter.

Past its initial terror, bravery feels like freedom. When I am brave enough to hope in the midst of unknowns and love past the point of heartbreak, I feel soft and serene, like an infant fresh from the tumult of birth on the chest of its mother. When I am brave, I reverberate with aliveness.

A few nights ago, I practiced one small act of bravery. I went to the "Soul Night" communal gathering hosted by my new church. This act of bravery tired me out. I felt awkward and worn out, and I had to leave early. As I was leaving, I thought to myself, *"I don't know if it was worth it."* The exact moment I thought that, I happened to look over and see the building I parked next to was painted with a giant mural. It read, "You are exactly where you need to be." So, there you have it. Maybe the middle—the waiting, hoping without seeing, and bravery that feels excruciating, is exactly where I need to be.

PART III
NEW PROMISES

HOW TO CARRY A BABY

I remember driving home from Los Angeles the weekend after Kyle moved into his new apartment. During the week, we had discussed what we wanted, where we wanted to go, and what we each believed. He did not want the same things as I did anymore. My heart felt both numb and anxious. I wondered how to tie my life to a man who was growing away from me. Most hauntingly, I wondered how I could have so wholeheartedly believed that he was the man for me if this was going to happen. That night, I went to the grocery store and sitting in my parked car, I had a meltdown. I remember praying aloud, through thick tears, "What did I do, God?"

All the dreams, impressions, and things that had seemed such compelling indications that my love for Kyle would be safe, growing to become a lifelong partnership—had I been wrong about them? I expressed these thoughts to God and went inside. As I shopped, this phrase kept rolling into my mind with precision clarity: "Do it again." Every time I began to feel anxious, these words came to my mind, "Do it again." As I paid for my groceries, I remembered that this was the name of a song and I thought I should probably listen to that song.

As I drove home, I played the song and heard a story about waiting for the completion of promises we expect to have already been fulfilled in our lives. I heard a story of trusting God's faithfulness as we wait to see breakthrough, knowing He has already accomplished the breakthrough. The chorus sang about God's promise remaining; that despite what we see, His words will prove true. Over and over, in this song, I heard the affirmation: God's promise remains.

The words of that song became bittersweet over the rest of my relationship with Kyle. When I first heard them, I swallowed my fear and loved Kyle with everything I had, until we disintegrated—until there was nothing of "us" left to love. When we fell apart, I mostly avoided those lyrics because they felt like a knife to the heart, something painfully confusing. These letters are the story of how I began to re-engage with the promise the words of that song spoke of. This is the story of how I grew the promise of new life—carrying it inside me like a baby, with expectancy and nurture.

DREAMS

The day after I reached out to Kyle in February, inspired by the white tulips, we talked for the first time in a long time. I can still remember the pictures he secretly took of me during that conversation. I think that they are some of the prettiest pictures of me that have ever been taken. I was not wearing anything special nor was the lighting particularly advantageous, but I looked happy: brave, alive, and glowing with love. In our relationship, Kyle usually initiated. He would pour out his love, intentions, and hopes. I would silently soak them in without much reciprocation. This day was different. On this day, I read Kyle a love letter that I had written him months before. In it, I asked him to come home to his heart.

In some ways, I think that is how God desires us humans to live all of the time: brave, alive, and overflowing with love. The caveat is that, although love makes us brave, here on earth, love also hurts. Loving bravely will inevitably accrue some damages; cultivating a heart that can hold and overflow with brave love is a challenge. On the way, you learn to hold sadness, disappointment, bitterness, anger. And then, learn to release them to make room for more love.

When I asked Kyle to come home to his heart, I dreamt one of the biggest, most beautiful dreams I could possibly imagine. The most difficult part of losing that dream was not the loss itself. It was repositioning my heart to receive life after loss. It was permitting myself to dream again; to hope for new love again, when all I wanted to do was recoil in fear of another disappointment. Learning to do so was terrifying but exhilarating—it meant living on the edge between another crushing heartbreak, and the explosion of my life and future.

The day I read Kyle that letter, I felt life to the fullest because I was loving despite the risk. There is something about loving despite the risk that makes us brave, alive, and overflowing with love. Strangely, it is only the power of love that rescues you from the pain of love. In opening your heart again, your heart expands. Your love becomes deeper, your brave becomes braver, and your dreams become bigger.

As I write this week, I have been unable to uproot this question from my head: what if the next big breakthrough in our lives, the new lives that come after grief, is waiting on the other side of trying one more time, showing up one more time, being vulnerable one more time? What if it is just beyond closing our eyes, taking a deep breath, and dreaming something wildly more spectacular than the dream that broke our hearts? We must choose love in this way. We must choose to open our hearts, over and over, day by day, again and again, because sometimes—the first step to a new life is a new dream. This is a letter I wrote one year after reading Kyle the letter asking to come home to his heart. In this letter, I gave voice to a new dream.

February 2018
DREAMS

Exactly one year after my February conversation with Kyle, the one in which I asked him to come home to his heart, I did something forward and bold, chasing down a dream I believed God gave me. I thought about how much had changed in a year, but I realized one thing had stayed the same. On that day in February, both this year and last, I did things that were bold.

Despite my recent acts of boldness, a new life has felt so far away. Instead of brave, I have felt alone, isolated, and forgotten. Last night I had difficulty falling asleep, so I played a podcast episode called *Incubation Through Isolation.*[1] This message used the Bible story of a man named Joseph to talk about how sometimes, what feels like isolation is actually incubation. Incubation is a season when things are developing with no outward indication of anything happening.

Joseph was a man with vivid dreams for his future, given to him by God. When he shared his dreams, it provoked jealously in his brothers to

---

1   Wilkerson, Rich Jr, Presenter. "Incubation Through Isolation." Vous Church. 21 Jan. 2018. https://itunes.apple.com/us/podcast/vous-church/id1042709241?mt=2

the extent that they planned to murder him, but instead ended up selling him into slavery. Through a long turn of events, he was taken to a country far from home, imprisoned, and eventually became second in command to the Pharaoh. Through these events, the realization of his dreams came to pass. The speaker made the parallel that seasons in life that feel isolating, like Joseph's time in prison, are actually incubation, preparing us for the grand delivery of all God's promises. As uncomfortable as these seasons are, we need incubation so that our lives and promises are not delivered prematurely.

Coming out of this recent season, I kind of just accepted that my dreams for my life would not come to pass. I rolled over and stopped asking for what I desired, assuming the answer would always be no. Yet, one thing I love about Joseph, is how he persisted in the very area where he seemed to have failed. Joseph was given a dream and because of it, he was sold into slavery and ended up in prison. If that had happened to me, I would have thought that I failed. I would have thought that I misunderstood God and the answer to my dream was "no." Not Joseph, he persisted in faith until God brought victory to his life.

Last night, I watched a tv show where one of the characters was pursuing his dream by opening a restaurant. To impress his investor, he decided to try a soft opening months before the restaurant was supposed to be ready. He tried to rush his dream.

The opening ended up being a disaster and as a result, he thought his dream was over. His friends however, would not let him quit, telling him that he had to keep going. This reminds me of my dreams. I do not want to rush their perfect timing. I want to wait for them to become what they need to be. Just because they are incubating and not happening now, does not mean they are the wrong dreams. And God is my friend, speaking into all that feels devastated and stagnant, saying, "Don't give up on the dreams for your new life; they just aren't ready yet."

More and more, I believe that beyond waiting, most dreams require persistence. Like a baby in the womb requires nine months of nurture before it is ready to be birthed, many dreams also require waiting with *intention*. This morning, I heard someone say that God wants us to persistently ask Him for the things we desire—that "no" today does not mean "no" tomorrow and we need to keep asking until God changes what we desire or fulfills our requests.[2]

It made me think about another story in the Bible, one that seems to keep popping up in the books I read and the podcasts I listen to. This story is about a man named Jacob, who was always trying to make his dreams come true through his own cleverness. One night, Jesus came down as a man and wrestled with Jacob. From that point on, Jacob was blessed. Even

2   Wilkerson, Rich Jr., Presenter. "The Art of Bothering God." Vous Church. 26 Nov 2017. https://itunes.apple.com/us/podcast/vous-church/id1042709241?mt=2

though Jacob made a lot of mistakes in pursuing his dreams, God loved his tenacity. With this story, I felt God encouraging *my* tenacity—the way I wrestle through with Him the dreams I believe He has given me, and how those are filled with question marks. He likes the way I ask for things and the way I am unafraid to dream big with Him. Like they did for Joseph, God given dreams often require aggressively pursuing, past the doubt in our own hearts and obstacles in our own lives, what is in the heart of God to give us. Dreams require bravery because they are often birthed in labor.

Carrying dreams in the situation with Kyle required so much intention—I held on and fought for our dreams until God released me. And it felt like labor. In feeling like I failed those dreams, I have wanted to give up on dreaming entirely. Yet, I have to keep the womb of my heart open to the new dreams I feel God whispering to me. I have to allow myself not just to dream, but to dream big. In the message about Joseph, the speaker mentioned that you should have some dreams so big and dependent on God, that they would be laughable to anybody else who heard them[3]. That is how I feel about the way that I dream.

The scary thing about dreams is that God places them inside our own heads and often they sound

3   Wilkerson, Rich Jr., Presenter. "God Dream: Don't Take No For an Answer" Vous Church. 14 Jan 2018. https://itunes.apple.com/us/podcast/vous-church/id1042709241?mt=2

awfully similar to our own thoughts. But God's thoughts are not our thoughts, and so He gives us dreams: thoughts we would never think up on our own. Thoughts He confirms with whispers— with timely Scriptures, songs, or television shows, with "coincidence" after coincidence, with our lives unfolding around these ideas in tiny but undeniable ways. The only things distinguishing our dreams from God's are an intimate familiarity with God's voice and a heart position of total surrender for the when and how.

There was nothing special about Joseph's dreams. They were natural dreams like the ones I have at night. There was no angel, writing in the sky, or any other grand revelation that assured him they were from God. They likely seemed more like the wishful thinking of a teenage boy than divine inspiration. Yet, Joseph discerned the subtle breath of God upon them. The same can be true for me.

I love the way the Scriptures talk about God's word and Jesus' voice. One of the Greek words used often to describe the word of God actually refers to spoken word, like the dialogue you would have with a friend. Another word used to describe the voice of Jesus, in its original language, refers to the sound and tone of that voice. Both of these words imply a nuanced recognition that requires intimacy. This February, as I remember the bold ways I have dreamt in the past, I do not have to be afraid of the seeming impossibility of my new dreams because they did not originate from me. They are *His* dreams placed in my heart, and I need to intentionally carry them.

This morning, the image of childbirth came to mind. Over and over, I have circled back to the way I feel about my situation with Kyle: stillbirth. This morning, the image of twins appeared in my heart. Kyle and I always talked about having physical twins. My dad was a twin, but his twin was stillborn. As I pondered these things this morning, I felt like God reminded me of twins—one living and one dead. In the past (before modern medicine gave us C-sections), when a woman was giving birth to twins, she had to continue delivering even if her first child was stillborn. To deliver the living child, she had to keep pushing. She could not stop because the first delivery ended differently than hoped for. She had to keep going so that the other child could be delivered. I feel like that applies to this situation. I cannot stop asking, dreaming, believing, and pressing in for the dreams and life God has given me because I am tired. I have to keep engaging in the process with hope, so that the dreams He has planted inside me can come to full term fruition.

I have spent my whole life afraid of God's "no." It has been ingrained in me by religion and my own fear of disappointment, that when you ask God for something you are likely to get a "no." When you dream something it most likely comes from your crooked little heart and not His will. I do believe in God's "no"—that sometimes He says it and when He

174

does, it is not so much as, "you better listen"—you just genuinely want to. Yet spending my whole life obsessed with His no has left me living life afraid to dream and believing in a God too small for a "yes."

In this season, I feel God calling me out of that. I feel all of my religious filters falling off, like clothes before a hot shower. Underneath, I am left with the naked truth of God's own Scriptures, which explicitly state that when we are intimate with Him, He gives us His dreams, His heart, His mind, and the ability to begin distinguishing those things from our own.

If this is true, fear is the only thing keeping me from believing that some of the wild, wonderful things occupying my imagination are from God. Am I brave enough to believe that even more intimately than I knew Kyle's breath, I can know God's? I can recognize it in a word or a dream or a thought? And if God gives me a dream, who am I to *not* carry it?

In this season, I will hold onto new dreams confidently and continue to ask God for good things until He blesses me. And I think He will, because this morning when I walked into church, we sang *Do It Again.*

PROMISES

Today, I had writer's block. So, I went to the beach. I live two minutes from a beach and only five minutes from my favorite beach. Yet, I did not want to go because I knew I needed to work on my book. I did not want to go because with the effort I perceived it would take to slide into sandals and walk out the door, you would think I had to go through customs to get to the beach. Nevertheless, I went because something deep inside me knew that the story that needed to be told, would be birthed if I walked on the sand.

I was right—something happens to me when I go to the beach. I find wonder in the midst of mundane life. One of the things I love most about the ocean is the million ways it reminds me of God. I love that the ocean is the most spectacular, beautiful, deep, expansive, all-encompassing, mysterious power you could imagine. It barrels toward the shore as if it is going to overtake you, and it could, but it stops. It stops and invites you to go deeper, to pause and stare, to respond. This happens day after day, night after night. This cycle, unlike the waves themselves, never stops. But I rarely do. In my own backyard are some of the most endless tones of blue you could imagine, some of the most melodious whispers of waves to the shore, some of the warmest sunshine you could curl up and sleep under. So often, I am barreling past this on the freeway because I have errands to run, work to finish, and traffic to beat, forgetting that some of the world's most glorious splendor is happening right beneath my nose.

I see promises as something like that. As I opened my heart to hope, new promises began trickling into my life but they sometimes felt dissonant, disconnected, and almost imperceptible. Reading back the collection of promises in this letter, they honestly still feel that way, a little bit. They can feel more like a grocery list than poetic food for the soul. I struggled over whether these promises were even worth writing about.

I decided they were when I went to the beach. Like the tide that pulls you out to deeper water, these promises pulled me into larger promises, hopes, and dreams. But I had to stop. I had to notice them. If my heart had not been open to finding wonder in the mundane, extravagance in ordinary, I would have missed them. So, I feel they must be included in my series of letters, because often, the process is piecing together everything that glimmers. Whatever that looks like for you: a song, something you read, a movie you watched, a walk on the beach. Stop. Find wonder. Find new promises.

March 2018

PROMISES

Sometimes it feels like life unfolds in themes, like it is writing itself into a story that I do not yet understand. Two days after writing about dreams incubating through isolation, like a baby in the womb, I woke to these inspiring words from my friend. She wrote, "Your miracle is coming." With her words, she paired a passage of Scripture about a great man of God, John the Baptist, and his miraculous conception. She shared that this story of miraculous conception could teach us about our own miracles. She wrote of John the Baptist's mother, Elizabeth, a woman who suffered barrenness, carrying with her the ensuing cultural shame. Upon her son's conception, she became a woman who carried her baby in seclusion. So, it seems as though my life right now is pregnant with the promise of things longed for, of miraculous things. Yet, I am carrying these promises in a quiet seclusion that is maturing them.

Like Elizabeth, I too have been feeling unseen and isolated, like I am carrying the hope for the next season alone. I am carrying hope for the next season adjacent to shame over the failure of the past season. In the moments between exciting encouragements, I struggle. I struggle with grief, feeling judged, thinking about Kyle being happy with other girls, and with everyone around me getting pregnant, having lives, and moving on. Doubt collects in the corners of my heart and I wonder if my life will really change in perceptible ways, if I will experience a relational rebirth, better than what I lost with Kyle. At the same time, I let myself declare, even in a whisper, that I believe in a new future. Maybe this is part of the miracle. Maybe right now, the miracle is not a new relationship or being seen in miraculous ways. Perhaps it is the steady strength to conceive a new dream and carry a new promise—to show up each day and let it grow a little bigger, a little stronger, silently inside of me.

My friend also wrote that she believes those who have been in seclusion for five months (since October, when my grieving process began) will begin to be revealed to the world in greater measure, in these next months of March and April. This makes me think of the man who delivered the message about incubation in isolation. Currently, his church is conducting a series of messages entitled "Miracle in Motion." In the middle of this series, his son was born, which is a real-life miracle in motion since this man and his wife struggled to conceive for eight years. As I find myself in the eighth year since I met Kyle, eight years filled with longing, heartache, and waiting for my life to burst forth, I sense in my heart a promise: the announcement of a season where emotional barrenness is rolled away, and my miracle is delivered.

Yet I am reminded that seclusion and revelation can only co-exist in dynamic motion. What I mean to say is that my miracle, like pregnancy, is here but has not fully arrived. As I carry the promises for my life, my very own miracle is in motion, growing and developing into something that I will see and feel take shape before me. Maybe other people are beginning to see that too because morning after morning, I am waking to words from friends saying things like, "God will heal you of the shame you feel," and "He will restore what you lost in doubled portions," and "look forward to a time of promises fulfilled."

Tonight, I listened to a message my mom sent me about God breaking off seven-year cycles of delay. The speaker shared that February was a time to experience these words that have been so special to me, since I first heard them on the day after my intended wedding: "(God) will make Trouble Valley a door of Hope."[1] Like my friend, the speaker felt that March and April would be special months, times for opportunities to open up, for delay to end and dead dreams to be resurrected. The speaker felt March 8th, specifically, would be a day of shift. I literally yelled out loud when I heard this because last night, in praying about my situations of disappointment, I had this quiet impression on my heart, that something significant would be birthed on March 8th. In my very uneventful life, I am learning to lean into the depth and breadth of the spirit inhabiting these ordinary things, and in them, find promise. Today, I thought

---

1   From Hosea 2:15 Good News Translation

about the three eights I saw on the building across from me on the day of my "New Era." March eighth is another combination of 3/8, another symbol of a new era—a springtime realization of a fresh start. So, I hold a promise that something as ordinary as a day on the calendar can be important.

I keep praying, what does March 8th hold for me? After praying about that this morning, I fell back to sleep and dreamt. When I awoke from my dream, I felt a strong impression on my heart to read a chapter in the Bible, specifically Ezekiel 39. I did not know what this chapter was about, so I looked it up. It is a chapter written to a nation in exile and it foretells a day when this country will be restored from its exile, by God's own sacrifice. The eighth verse of this passage reads, "It's coming! Yes, it will happen! *This* is the day I've been telling you about."[2] Maybe March 8th is a promise of no more delay, an assurance that *today* is the day of God's promise.

In the book of Ezekiel, God promises this day of hope and follows it up by directing that a new temple be measured out, in the nation's 25th year of exile. Temples in the Scripture are often used to describe the old and new works of God. They were cultural symbols of God's presence and prosperity, for which God's people yearned. The temple that had preceded this new one had taken seven years to build and then was destroyed.

---

2   Ezekiel 39:8 The Message, Emphasis added

I feel tension in this season. It is a time of seclusion and a time of revelation. A time of now and a time of not yet. A time to anticipate what is coming and a time to receive what is already here today. A time of promise. I think promise, pregnancy, and building things from devastation are all like that. They are moments equally full of tangible vision and uncertainty over the future. In these moments, even as you are waiting, you are building and growing toward the vision. Sometimes in these moments, a promise is all you have. More often than we think, that is enough. Maybe that thing growing deep inside me through promise, is the very thing I need to grow and unfold into a new life. Maybe the new life and promise is not so much something out there, but something here in my heart. Maybe it is not so much something I need to discover, but something I need to grow.

At the time I wrote this letter, all I could see restoration to look like was finding who would replace Kyle. Looking back, I see I was looking for one promise of my heart to be fulfilled when instead, my whole life was morphing into a promise. It was not just my relationship that was being called out of exile, it was my whole life. The land I was being called into was the spiritual land of a life rich with promise, hope, depth, and fullness. For so long, when I was with Kyle, my heart had been banished from fully inhabiting this richness. Slowly, I was being called out of emotional exile. I was being called into my own emotional space. I was being called into a life big enough for my growing, developing heart, into a life that fit the person growing deep inside of me. And promise after promise, my heart, my place of devastation, was re-birthed, rebuilt, and restored.

SEEDS

March was another letting go...

I remember the first cup of coffee I had with a man after Kyle and I broke up. It was over a year after our relationship ended, after everything I have written about in this book had already transpired. It was not really romantic, just a cup of coffee with a friend of a friend. We met in the evening after work; it was winter and cold outside, even in San Diego. When I entered the coffee shop, he was sitting in the back, already sipping on a green tea latte concoction. We made small talk as I unwrapped myself from my coat and scarf. Once I had ordered my drink, we sat down to talk. It was nothing like my first coffee with Kyle had been. This stranger and I talked conversationally and amicably, for an hour at most. When it was over, we chatted on the way to our cars, briefly hugged in the brisk night air and went our separate ways. I felt disappointed. I had built this meeting up so much in my head: we would hit it off and talk for hours, only to be followed by magnetic attraction that led to a series of dates and inevitably marriage. I realize now that this sounds fanciful and delusional, but the crazy thing is—that is what had happened with Kyle. Exactly. We met and what came next was immediate, red-hot pursuit. This time as I drove home from the coffee shop, I told God I felt disappointed and I heard in response these words from *The Chronicles of Narnia*, "Things never happen the same way twice."[1] I began to wonder if maybe slow was better. Perhaps something different, new, and a little deeper, grew from a process. I wondered if something good came from letting go of expectations, letting them fall into the slow-moving reality of what is.

March was something like that. For seven long months since my breakup with Kyle, I was waiting for my life to resume. It felt like my plans had been put on pause and I was waiting to jump back into relationship, engagement, marriage, and the whole kids-house-golden retriever thing with someone else, at any moment. When I heard words of hope about March, the ones I received as promises, I anticipated that something grand would happen. The new relationship was almost here, just around the corner, ready to be delivered. My whole life was going to spring up in one explosive event.

What happened instead was releasing and transforming. A few days before March, I prayed that God would help me be a blank canvas. Immediately after I prayed that, I read words Song had written about how God's thoughts are not our thoughts and if we want to see the miracles of March, we have to lay down our

---

1   C.S. Lewis, "Prince Caspian" in "The Chronicles of Narnia"

expectations, offering our minds and hearts to him as "blank."

The letting go did not happen all at once. It was more the dawning of a slow realization. It was me uncurling gradually into the recognition that what I had expected for March and all I had expected for the new season of my life, might not happen exactly as I had expected or might not happen at all. But in the softness of those disappointed expectations, there were different things to be found. In letting go, there were seeds of life.

March 2018

SEEDS

It is hard to write about a process while you are still in it. I wrote this beautiful letter about process. It was full of metaphors and insights, but when I read it back it felt totally wrong. It felt stale, like day old pastry. I think it was because I was writing about beautiful conclusions without actually coming to them myself. I have been trying to write about a process while being stuck in it myself.

My expectations for March were something totally different than what is playing out. I expected a dramatic shift. And nothing has happened. Day after day goes by on the calendar without anything different or new. There is breakfast, class, and my usual routine. At first, I began to think that all the things I heard about March were not going to come true after all. In the wake of that, the word "small" began to trickle into my cognizance. I have seen it on billboards and tea bags, hearing it in messages too. "It is a season for small things." "Appreciate small beginnings." These words are whispering a new wonder to me: perhaps the significant things I have been looking for are happening in all that is small and "routine" in my life.

Recently, I began thinking about a story from the life of Jesus; about a paralyzed man, lying by a healing pool. Jesus asked this man if he wanted to be healed and the man told Jesus that he did, but that there was nobody to help him into the healing pool. I wondered—was this his way of asking Jesus for what he wanted? For help getting into the pool? In response, Jesus told him to take up his mat and walk. Not exactly the answer he was probably expecting. This man had been waiting 38 years for healing from this pool. In that moment, he had to choose to trust Jesus. He had to immediately leave behind hopelessness, doubt, disappointment, and *an expectation of where his miracle would come from.* What struck me most about this story is that this man brought his expectations to Jesus. He had a vision of healing from this pool, and Jesus called him to something different. To walk into the healing he had truly been longing for all those years he had to recalibrate his mindset about where his miracle would come from. He had to trust that his miracle came from God—not a pool or any other specific thing.

If I am honest, I struggle to let go of my visions for the future. I feel like God gave me some specific dreams and encouraged me to ask for them. Now, it seems He is asking me to let them go, which is so painful. Maybe letting go of expectations does not mean that the vision is wrong. For the man at the healing pool, his vision was not wrong. He wanted healing and Jesus wanted to give him healing, but in order to receive it, he had to surrender to how God chose to accomplish it. It made me wonder if I have been looking to the vision instead of God to heal me. I have all along thought healing would come from a new relationship, one that would make everything that happened with Kyle okay. I thought that healing would come through something epic and life changing. But it seems that God is calling me into something different, something smaller.

I talked to my mom about how I have been feeling. She said, "I think during this time, you'll have a process of becoming your own person. You may have had hopes that your actions would facilitate some kind of outcome, but now maybe God is teaching you to let Him complete His process in you, which is not seeking your own way. 'Unless a seed falls to the ground and dies, it will not bear fruit.'[2] Maybe, letting these seeds fall to the ground and die, will be the very thing that helps them grow." When she said that, I thought about how seeds yield

---

2   John 12:24

beauty that is created through a process, and each step of that process is invaluable to the completed vision. Development through process requires letting go and right now, that feels like suffocating the only small pieces of life I have left to hold.

Perhaps underneath all that letting go, there is a deeper healing for me, one in which I understand my healing comes from God and not a man—that even when things are undone, not stitched up and nicely healed, God is still my healer. He is still good, He is still trustworthy, even in the messy process. I can sit in broken-hearted, disappointed, and missed expectations and still be healed. My healing does not come from the outcome of a situation.

It reminds me of the verse Song wrote about on the day Kyle and I got back together for the last time. "Come, let us return to the Lord. He has torn us to pieces, but He will heal us; He has injured us, but He will bind up our wounds. After two days He will revive us; on the third day He will restore us, that we may live in his presence."[3] I never understood that verse. I did not like the idea of God tearing us to pieces, but now I get it. Maybe the healing only comes with the ripping and tearing—the uprooting and releasing of things that we have kept tightly guarded for so long, thinking if we did not have them we would not be able to breathe. Maybe when the wounds are still gaping open and the expectations

---

3   Hosea 6:1-2 New International Version

are unmet, that is when real healing happens. It is not the healing I had envisioned, but it is a better and more complete healing.

So here I am, without the happy ending I thought would make everything okay. Instead, I am facing a process where things in me need to be opened and changed, in order for the things I desire to come to life. This process is small, but it is changing everything. Letting go of my grasp on what I hope for most is the very thing that is handing back to me what I desire most—love. This process teaches me to lay down my will to another's, to God's will, something at the very heartbeat of love. Up to this point, I have loved with expectations of God and others—expectations that if I lived and loved a certain way, God and others would somehow interact to bring me everything I wanted. In the face of all that, the process says "surrender." Letting go might be how these seeds will grow. Maybe time will make them more beautiful and going deep will make them come alive.

So, maybe, this is grace.
When I find myself at the place,
Where things seem to be falling apart, instead of falling together.
Maybe sometimes, things need to break
So that other things may break through.

The morning after I wrote this, I woke to the first day of spring.

GRATITUDE

I never thought I was a big diamond lady until Kyle suggested I try on a 3-carat diamond. I now like big diamonds. I remember the way it looked on my finger. It gleamed clean and elegant, a sparkling reminder that my man thought I was worth a $12,000 rock. I saw rings everywhere after Kyle and I broke up, and they left this strange sense of emptiness in my heart. It felt like a rock, but the kind in the bottom of your stomach and not the beautiful kind on your finger. I tried attending a women's group a few days after we stopped talking, and I think I would have felt more inconspicuous wearing a $15,000 ring than how I felt that night in a room full of married peers.

Not long after we broke up, the engagement ring company sent me promotional mail. It was a coupon for 20% off your next order. I cried, thought of who I could give it to, and eventually threw it away. A few weeks later, they sent me another one—straight to the trash. By the time the third one came, I found the courage to call Brilliant Earth and ask them to remove me from their mailing list. "Would you like to be on our email list?" No, I would not.

Though all I could feel was a hollowness, whenever I saw a wedding or engagement ring, I was experiencing shame. I felt unworthy of something beautiful and expensive like a diamond. We often call that sensation of emptiness grief, but more often, it is a series of feelings masquerading as grief. Feelings like anger, bitterness, disappointment, and rejection.

Through the process, I learned that in some ways, life is like a diamond. Some days it appears brilliant and shiny, full of earthy wonder. Other days, it feels awfully like a rock. This letter reminds me that in the emptiness of grief, I began to feel some brilliant things too. I felt gratitude, filling the holes Kyle had left behind.

March 2018

GRATITUDE

Lately I have been feeling empty. At times, this has triggered grief and at other times, panic. After Kyle and I broke up, I possessed a deep peace that I would meet someone and enter into another relationship soon. This feeling allowed me to avoid the emptiness of truly being without a relationship. Yet time is ticking on and in the absence of a new relationship, the emptiness is creeping up and I feel panic. *What if a new relationship never comes?*

For as long as I can remember, it has seemed like the purpose of my life was to get married. My grandmother was left by her husband on Valentine's Day—it traumatized her and left me with the strong impression that securing a man was very important. As soon as I was old enough to dress up, I dressed up like a bride, piecing together anything white or lacy from our garage sale costume box into something loosely resembling a bridal gown. Watching *Cinderella* made me believe in love at first sight and I used to do my chores singing *Someday My Prince Will Come.* I did not care about career aspirations; I wanted to grow up to become a wife and a mom. At five or six years old, the purity of these desires was defiled when I got a little experience doing what married people do. Even at such a young age, I intuitively knew that the person doing those things to me was supposed to love me and stay with me after it was over. He did neither of those things and *I felt shame.* From that moment on, the desire became a need. I have not been able to imagine a life in which I do not experience a man choosing me and protecting me and, from that love, growing family. I have needed it to heal the experience of a man violating me and discarding me and, from that experience, being ostracized from community. I went my whole life waiting for someone to love me the way I thought Kyle was going to love me—to prove that I was worthy of love. This hope did not dissolve when my relationship with Kyle ended but has simply been suspended in time.

Recently, I heard this question posed: *if your hopes never come to pass in the way you thought they would, will you worship God anyway?* When I reflect on this question, I think of how worship goes beyond singing a song. Worship is allowing my emotions to be overtaken by a spirit filled with joy and thankfulness for the abundance of what I have today, instead of focusing on what I do not have. In light of that, I am asking myself: if I never find a partner to love again, if I never grow my own children inside my body, *am I willing to be happy?*

Honestly, I have been struggling with saying yes to that question. It is a massive letting go of all the expectations and hopes I have held for my life. It leads me to more questions: what if I always sleep alone? What if there is no one to hold me again? What if physical affection is not part of my life, and if being thought of as beautiful is not an affirmation I receive? These thoughts have left me with a terrible feeling of emptiness; a deep, longing hollowness for all the things I loved about being with Kyle.

The thing is, I like good men. I liked how having a good man (or at least a man) of my own made me feel seen, loved, and protected. I loved the dynamic of being pursued and responding by nurturing the person who pursued me. I love to call out life in good men, helping them open their hearts to their fullest potentials. I think of my life without any of that and I feel so overlooked, unimportant, unattractive, and unknown. I feel rejected by men and I want to be accepted by them.

I have struggled with a willingness to be happy without all these things because I am afraid of losing the *desire* for them. I feel afraid that if I allow myself to be happy without possessing what I desire, these things will no longer be priorities to me. I am afraid of forgetting how amazing it feels to be held, how tenderly open and fully alive my heart is when giving my all to become one with someone. I am afraid of forgetting how special it is to connect with someone in 1,000 little ways throughout the day, to feel aligned in being seen. I am afraid of forgetting that I can be adored. I feel like the desire for these things and the belief that they can exist again, in an even purer way, is too valuable to shut down. But maybe, I am not supposed to shut them down. There is a verse in the Bible that talks about not going further than God has asked you to. As I wrote down questions about *"what if I never"*... the verse came to mind and I felt that, in this season, God is not asking me to discard these desires but to be a good steward of them.

Gratitude is a key to stewarding well. *Am I willing to be thankful, even if everything is not the way I want it?* Can I trust God's heart, without judging His intentions? Can I believe that His desire is to fill me with good things, when my experience feels like a withholding of good things? Less than all of this, am I able and willing to just try?

It is not so much about extinguishing the desires or the grief as much as it is about holding space for them, and allowing them to co-exist with gratitude and uncertainty—to let gratitude become joy and to allow myself to feel joyful, even if I do not know where it will lead. Maybe, it is about learning to find and feel value when my life does not live up to my expectations, when I feel like I am missing the mark for where I should be at this age, and when I feel left out of community because I do not have a partner or a family of my own. When I feel unimportant to people, am I willing to have the courage to "show up" to life? Even if I perceive that nobody notices or cares? *Can I value a life that is my own?* I think learning to do so is vitally important. Jesus died and rose from His grave to dignify my life. He took on undignified shame to demonstrate that my life is worthy. Maybe, He is allowing me to wrestle with shame in this season so that I may truly arrive at the realization of my worth.

Today, I wrote out a manifesto of sorts. I thought of God as my Father and made a list of the ways He desires me to understand I am worthy. These notes remind me that when I have gratitude and give thanks, I can see how the things in my life that feel empty and void are actually places of richness. They are the places where I am learning to engage with worth and engage with the world. These words are my vision for right now—my reminders of the purpose of this season and all I can lean into when I do not want to do the hard work of being here:

God wants me to love myself as He loves me. He wants me to feel deeply and bleed love, from a place inside my soul that welcomes my shortcomings and approves of myself despite my imperfections. He wants me to recognize my value, *independent of any other human being's approval* and He wants this to translate into a gentle, quiet confidence from which I engage with the world. He wants me to value the process that forges this, the perseverance it calls for, and the respect it instills in me for others' processes. He is okay with me sitting in the unseen, unknown, and overlooked, because He does not want me to be afraid of this place but to transform it. Because when I transform it, I can float. I can move with a resilience and bravery that makes me strong and free. And for all of that, I am saying "thank you."

LEARNING TO BE RESCUED

When the month of April arrived, I decided not to re-sign the lease at my apartment. When your whole life has been shaken up and you have lost the past seven years as well as your future (what you thought would be the next forever years)—why not shake things up a little more? Why not also lose the one secure thing in your life - a steady place to live? Even bolder, I decided to live alone for the first time. Although I was excited about this adventure, it presented some challenges.

Living on my own was exponentially more expensive than living with another person. In a competitive rental market, the apartment I applied for was taken by someone else and I had nothing lined up when my moving date came. With no family nearby, I had to pack up a two-bedroom apartment all by myself. The whole endeavor became completely overwhelming. It amplified the sense of loneliness I had felt in Kyle's absence. My mind often wandered to how easy it would be to drive up to his house and ask to sleep on his couch.

What made this situation worse is that I faced not just these few, but many challenges in finding a place to live. I thought I might need to stay with friends for a month, at the very worst. In total, I ended up living house to house, sleeping on couches, floors, and guest beds, living out of the trunk of my car, for nearly half a year. There is nothing that makes you grasp the reality of your singleness than a situation like that. I was a girl with a suitcase and boxes of clothes in the back of my car, floating from house to house, being taken care of by married friends. I was discovering a whole new world without Kyle. I was doing something that never would have happened if we were together—something I assumed he would have been decidedly against. I was doing things on my own, discovering a world that was totally new, a little terrifying, and pretty unorganized. I tried to spin it romantically to myself: it was nomadic and adventurous. It was. It was also exhausting.

I remember nights lying awake with a severe sense of panic, wondering where I would sleep the next week and longing for help. I longed for a partner to help me qualify for an apartment, help me move heavy boxes, and to rescue me from the unknown and alone. What I was looking for never came. I think this is one of the best things that could have happened to me after losing Kyle. In the quiet, little space of my apartment and my heart, I had been learning to have light on my own. Through moving and being seen as vulnerable by a lot of different people, through stepping into a situation that demanded fierce independence and interdependence, that light was forced to grow, expand outward, and build. From the light of my own grew a life of my own. I could ask for no better rescuing than that.

ON MY OWN

I want to be rescued. I am beginning to believe that this is a deep human need. In the past few weeks, I have been transitioning out of my current housing situation, by my own choice. Yet, due to other people's choices and circumstances beyond my control, the transition has been a little rockier than I hoped. I took a risk, deciding not to renew my lease before I had new housing guaranteed, and all the little pieces remain suspended in the unknown instead of coming together as I had hoped. I feel fear and panic, with something that runs even more deeply beneath both.

I feel the same drowning, throat tightening sensation that I always feel when I try to express my needs and no one responds. A feeling I experience when I am trying to stand up for myself and it does not seem to do any good, when no one cares to help me, even if I advocate for myself. In my life, there is no Kyle to help me catch all the moving pieces and arrange them into something that feels safe and secure. There is no one to stand up for me or protect me from the unknown. All that I have is my own voice, which I feel has been ineffective before and seems to be the same now. All I can do is use that voice and hope it brings about change in some of the ears it falls on.

This situation reveals to me the uncomfortable truth that I have unfinished business in this season: the business of learning to navigate life, without depending on a person to rescue me, and learning to become strong. I see in this intense sensation of helplessness which has surfaced in Kyle's absence, that I have perhaps never had a strength of my own. I have always been looking to another person to be strong for me and I have come to a point in my life where that is no longer an option. So now, I have asked God to rescue me. I have wanted Him to come down and sprinkle magic dust on all my problems so they evaporate into a beautiful place to live and a seamless transition. That has not happened, but what I know and am finding between anxious breaths, is that God is in this place and He is rescuing me in a totally different way than I asked for, in a way that leads to strength instead of ease. Here is how:

There is a Bible story they used to tell in Sunday school when I was a child. It was about a man named Jonah who ran away from God. Through a series of events, he ended up being swallowed by a whale. The story goes that he cried out to God for rescue from the belly of the whale, and was spit up onto dry ground. What makes this story so interesting is that Jonah was rescued so he could do the very thing he was running away from.

This makes me think that the problem with a desire to be rescued is not so much the desire itself, but what or who we look to to fulfill it. God wants us to feel comfortable asking Him to rescue us, not only because He is gentle and wants to help us in our needs, but also because He wants us to live lives beyond our own capabilities, which will certainly require help. Yet (as seen in the story of Jonah), God's rescuing more often looks like empowering us to face things we are afraid of, rather than removing them.

I experienced this the other day while feeling angry about the situations I want to be rescued from. In the depth of my emotions, I had this revelation: It is okay to feel angry. The disproportionate anger that I felt in the moment, was a somewhat misplaced feeling. I was feeling what I wanted someone to feel for me twenty years ago, when I was taken advantage of and it seemed like I did not matter to anyone because no one came to help. I think twenty years ago, God felt an anger like what I was feeling in this most recent moment.

In some ways, this anger is good. This anger over being ignored when I cry for help, never had a voice before. Experiencing it now in a safer context is helping me recognize the injustice of what was done to me years ago. It is okay to be angry (which is different from being bitter and unforgiving) over that injustice. When that feeling of anger is acknowledged and released, it can drive me to strength; enabling me to respond how I need to in desperate situations. Anger is my heart's way of telling me that I feel in danger, but I have the strength to defend myself. Anger is a God-given emotion and like Jonah's God-given rescuing, it is driving me to face situations I am afraid of. The problem with my anger is that currently, it is mixed with fear. I have been meditating on this verse "perfect love casts out fear"[1] and asking myself: what does love look like injected into this situation? Honestly, I think that love is standing up for *myself*—not emotionally exploding, but being willing to advocate for my needs regardless of the outcome. It is the bravery to do all the things that I wanted Kyle to do for me. As I bring love for myself into situations I fear, the fear will slowly begin to fade and the need to be rescued will transform.

Here in the love, God is challenging me to understand rescuing as something deeper. He is meeting my heart's craving for rescue by giving me a spiritual understanding of what it means to be rescued. I wanted something big and miraculous to shift this situation, but the answer and rescuing I was looking for, is right in front of me. It is in letting God's love wash over my human self and emotions, driving me to strength instead of fear and into action instead of hiding. As I take action from a place of believing I am loved, I will become stronger. I will learn that I can face the situations where I feel alone and unseen, without being afraid of them anymore.

I really do believe that God "rescues" in the classic sense of the word. Sometimes, He really does provide miraculous deliverance through the dramatic reversal

---

1   1 John 4:18 b New International Version

of a situation. I have seen Him do it before. Yet, I also think His deliverance is different in different circumstances. Sometimes His deliverance comes in teaching us how to walk through scary things in the strength of love so that the power of fear is nullified. His deliverance is teaching us how to overcome, because when we overcome, we take ownership of the love and strength He has for us. We live it, express it, and then regenerate it. We find ourselves in a totally different and better place than the one in which we started.

GOOD MEN

After Kyle and I broke up, I met a lot of accomplished and kind men. Occasionally one would catch my interest, although this did not happen often. When it did, I began to realize something. On so many of the men who were kind to me, I unconsciously but immediately wanted to place the burden of all my disappointed hopes and dreams—the expectations of a rebuilt future.

Yet one of the greatest lessons that I learned through loving Kyle, is that love has a choice. I wholeheartedly believe that over and over, God presents us with situations glittering with goodness. Equally, I believe that He never forces us to step into these situations. So it is with every man I will ever love. As much as I believe that God can prepare hearts for each other, I also believe that each heart has a choice in accepting an invitation to love another human. No matter how fervently I love a man, he will always have to choose to love me back. That is part of the agony of love. Some of the people you love will not love you back. That is also part of what makes love such a thrilling free fall. You jump, without a parachute, knowing that you will not be caught safely, every time you jump.

In my relationship with Kyle, I felt like I gave away my power. While I fought it consciously, the feeling that I would fail without him in my life seeped in. If the person I loved most in the world did not stand behind me or believe in me, did I have anything to offer or have the ability to succeed? I found a different dynamic with the men I met after Kyle. They did not love or want to date me. Not one of them was interested in experiencing me physically. They did not consider me an object to satisfy their desires. Instead, they respected me. They told me my words were important, built up my character, and encouraged my career path. They were good men. At first, I tried to stuff these good men into holes and boxes, and holes in boxes, like crayons. Little soldiers lined up and colored to fit the needs of my heart.

Through interactions with the good men I have met since breaking up with Kyle, I have come to realize that to place the burden of my hopes on another soul is not to love it, but to crush it. It is to disregard the element of that soul's choice in loving me. It is the act of crashing into the sacred places of another's heart, before truly knowing or understanding that heart. Love never invades. Love always invites. Love does not suck another's essence into the empty spaces of the heart. Instead, love overflows from my heart in a way that opens it to others—opens my heart to a true curiosity, understanding, regard without expectation, and an admiration without possession. Love invites another to step into that process with me, but never demands.

In some ways, this is my letter to all the good men out there. It is both an apology and a declaration that my hope for each one is that he chooses who he loves. My prayer for each of those men, for all of us really, is this: that the choices we make come from love and not fear.

April 2018

GOOD MEN

Today, as I conversed with my counselor Sarah, I thought about learning to be full on my own. Sarah used the word "process" with me—the word I had secretly chosen for the series of letters and reflections I have been writing in my journal. She told me that this process of grief I am going through is not "being stuck", but is my journey on the way to my next relationship. She said something so poignant: that, if the right person came into my life right now, it might not be the right time. Her words filled me with gratitude, reminding me that, in this process, I am learning how to have light on my own.

I am learning how to move toward relationships in interdependency instead of codependency. At my appointment today, I told Sarah about a moment in my move when the loneliness *suddenly* shifted. I was thinking of how deeply I desired help and, in the next instant, I realized that I could feel lonely even if Kyle was in my life. Loneliness is not about who is or is not in my life, but about the condition of my soul. In that moment, I also *felt* God helping me. His presence was validating my existence when no one else was. With that,

I was released from having to outsource the emotional caretaking of my heart.

When I am okay on my own, I am free to love without condition. I am free from trying to force or coerce another person into loving me. Here, I can finally see the good men because I can stop looking at them as the drain stops that fill all the holes in my leaking heart. I can see them for who they are, realizing that nobody can do the job of loving myself for me—a job I let Kyle do for me for far too long.

It is a little scary in this soft and gracious place, where I am learning that I cannot earn the future I hope for. I cannot earn the love or presence of a good man, as much as I was unable to earn the love of Kyle. Love can only ever be given. This is a heartbreaking thing to realize—that you can never earn another's love. It submerges you into the depths of yourself, into the vantage point where you see all the things you love about yourself and all the things others overlook in you, in the same shadow, in the same light. There is pain here, knowing some of the people you want to love you never will. Yet, there is also freedom, because once you understand that you can never earn another's love, you see that likewise you can never earn your *own* love. It can only be given without condition.

This letter reminds me that in order to see good men, I had to distill my process to the bare bones, unseen place. It was not until I reached this place that I gained the vantage point to see the good men who were always there. So, I think that finding good men was never about where they were. It has always been and will always be, about where my own heart is and who I know myself to be.

HOME

I remember the week Kyle moved into his Los Angeles apartment. He had been living in Las Vegas and moved to propose to me. We fought a lot that week. I was angry. He was angry. Nevertheless, he called me from Target the day after moving because he needed me. He did not know which shower curtain rings to buy. I talked him through the ropes, and I can still hear his voice whispering on the other end of the line—"This is why I need you, baby." I drove up the next day and tried to solve his domestic problems like why, after three days, there was still no soap in the house. We went to Ikea and shopped for furniture. We sat on all the couches and I tried to encourage him toward the rugs I would want to keep when it was our apartment and we played house. Except, it was not playing—it was happening. Him, me, us. Together, we were making a home.

Months later, I found myself on my own, preparing to move into my own empty space—no Kyle, no us, just me. To me, moving was symbolic of leaving behind the sense of home that I had found in Kyle's heart. I had already thrown away most of the relics of our relationship, like the little love notes stuffed in corners of my room. Yet, sifting through all my possessions was a deeper letting go. I found things like one of his socks and the ring sizer I had been keeping "in case I get engaged again." Throwing these away felt like tearing out hooks he still had in my heart. When I left, I left behind a thousand memories, like Kyle kissing me in the stairwell, looking at me with the biggest blue eyes you have ever seen, and asking me to come home to him. When I left, I knew that I would never "go home" to him again and he would never again "come home" to me.

With my moving onward there also happened a moving inward. I left home and found a new one. It was not one I found in Kyle, but one I learned to establish in my own heart, making and receiving it everywhere I went. I used to crave security—four walls that would stay in one place, walls that I could go home to, walls that would collect comforts like pictures and holiday decorations. In leaving those walls behind, I learned to crave an extraordinary life. On the road, while that new life was taking shape and felt more overwhelming than extraordinary, these were the words I wrote:

May 2018

HOME ON THE ROAD

I want a home. A place where I can lay in bed at the end of the day and be safe and known, feeling understood in the quiet darkness for who I am. No show, nothing impressive. Just me—skin and bones and breath, all interconnected by love. I do not know that I have felt that since my relationship with Kyle ended. Beneath all our dysfunction and the ways I was trying to force love, there were these spots of softness between us where he loved me like that. I think of the way he adored me in the old, holey t-shirts I would wear as pajamas, the way he cherished just being together while we brushed our teeth—the way he would hold me in the silence and dark when I was sad, angry at him, or afraid. It was these moments of wordless connection between us, where we understood, accepted, and loved each other just by being, that glued us together.

I do not have a physical home today. But today, I visited someone else's home. It was airy, beautiful, and near the sea—everything I had dreamed about building with Kyle. It reminded me that, even without Kyle, I so deeply long for home—a space of my own to make into a beautiful place of rest. A place where love can find you even at your simplest, most essential, most unimpressive self and glue all your fraying pieces back together.

My life feels like it is in a funny place right now. It feels like an adventure space, on the road. It is not a homey space or a restful place. It is more like camping. Every time it settles into one pattern, it seems like everything is shaken up anew. In the unpredictability and interim, my heart feels a little homeless. There is no banner over me advertising how drastically transformed my heart has been during this time and there is no season where my heart is yet settled.

Tonight, as I sleep on a futon mattress, I keep thinking over and over again how Jesus is my true home. Together, we are making a home inside of my heart, created from love—a place where I belong and where others can find love and belonging too. Maybe the transformation of my heart into a home means I will feel safe, secure, rooted, expansive, and beautiful in any situation. Maybe it means learning to be okay with growing a beauty that nobody sees, which feels disappointing. Maybe it means learning to be okay with how things are different. "Different" is a lot more unfinished than what I thought I wanted. It is more like a custom home under construction, than a track property with all the quick and shiny finishes that everyone else has. Slowly, I am learning to be okay with that— with unfinished, unsettled and homeless. In all of these spaces, the house of my heart is being constructed into something beautiful and deep. Though it is uncertain, I am finding shelter. Through all the unfinished cracks, love is finding a way in. In the open and unknown, I am finding my own; I am finding home.

Through the process, home became nothing but different. Home was built not with furniture or Ikea gift cards, but with asking for and letting people help; letting my heart expand into someone's life, someone's dinner table conversation, and letting myself be seen. Home was built not with one person, like Kyle, but with many people—people who supported my heart as it grew into curiosity and adventure, as it grew large. Though I did not realize it at the time, this was the truest process of letting love find my most broken self and glue me back together. It was not glamorous and romantic. It was gritty, real, unspoken love meeting me where I was at, softening all the jagged pieces of my broken heart and life. So, as I left behind four walls and the old life and relationship I thought I needed to feel safe and loved, I found something else.

I began to discover that there might be something beyond the steady, dependable walls of a house. Under the surface of a life that felt safe and predictable, there was something deep stirring. It was the unknown, unexplored, uncharted territory- and it was calling me.

In this space, home expanded into something new. It was not a floor and a roof. It expanded into sky, stars, grass, and earth. It expanded into feeling each fiber of these things, letting them fill my lungs. It expanded into finding love anywhere and carrying it always with me. Home became a practice, of opening my heart to the broad earth filled with good, kind people who wanted to come into my heart and remodel it into what I always wanted—a space of beauty and rest.

FORGIVENESS

During the period of my nomadic living, I attended a shower for a friend who had recently become engaged. Both the bride and groom were mutual friends of Kyle and I. They had become engaged in February, my lowest month following our breakup. This had not been easy for me as they held a similar story to ours, having met seven years prior. They knew they were meant for each other to the point of being engaged but, due to incompatibilities, they called off their engagement for several years. Like us, they had gotten back together and decided to get married and engaged quickly. When they became engaged, the groom talked about the death of relationships and spring rebirth leading to new life. That stung. It stung a little extra because I felt that with their engagement, all the people who had watched their relationship thrive and all the people who had watched my relationship die, would judge me. I felt like somehow, people did not believe my relationship with Kyle had been real— that I had not felt the same love, seen the same type of signs indicating we were meant to be together, or endured the same heartache for him that my friends had experienced for each other, leading them to marriage and us to break up.

That was how it often was with Kyle and I. When people could not understand us, they dismissed us. Although the bride and the groom were my friends, I felt more like a hand me down friend to them, one inherited through family relationships instead of for my own merit. Nevertheless, I was determined to be happy for them, and to avoid being swallowed alive by self-pity, grief, comparison, and a sense of failure. I sent the congratulations text when I heard of their engagement, and a few months later when the bridal shower came, I drove my house/car to attend.

The bridal shower took place in Los Angeles, where Kyle lived. I put on lipstick and my best romper, curled my hair to the nines, and felt the hollowness of being in a place that had been us, without Kyle. I ate cheese and raspberries, and made conversation about everyone's cute haircuts and how charming the decorations were. I sat next to the wife of Kyle's best friend and I was genuinely glad to see her because she is the sweetest person you can imagine. I wrote a heartfelt card and carried myself with all the dignity of a homeless ex-girlfriend, trying not to imagine how this would be my life if things were different. The bride told their love story, their seven, almost eight-year story of love, loss, and coming back together. Everyone ooed and awed over how "when you know you know" and how life sends you signs. I fought back tears because I had "known" and life had sent me signs too.

That day, I felt the similarities in the story more than the differences. I felt that this marriage and restoration could have been my story too, if I would have chosen it. Shortly before we finalized our breakup, Kyle asked me to go to the courthouse with him to be married. I told him, as I told him every time he asked me that question, no. No, because marriage was not a viable alternative to doing the hard work of solving our problems.

I made that choice with a deep knowledge of the challenges a life with Kyle would present. I made the choice for a different life. That choice was reached gradually, and continues to be made over and over, every day since our breakup. That choice was hard-fought and hard-won, in battles that were private, like all other elements of my process with Kyle.

Before I left, the bride told me that Kyle would be at the wedding. When I heard that, my heart started to fray a little. I had not expected that. I would be seeing Kyle in a few short weeks. My hard-fought choice suddenly felt vulnerable. I felt nervous and unprepared, like the heart change I had delivered so laboriously, would be exposed. I felt like I had delicately woven an intricate tapestry of the heart and someone had yanked out a string. How was I to keep my heart, emotions, and forward momentum from unraveling? I did not know, so I cried. As soon as I reached my car, I cried. I cried on the drive home and when I curled up in the guest bedroom of my host's home. I cried and let the emptiness gnaw its way out of my heart. I carried the grief and questioning through the week, from house to house. I let process take place and when something had formed, I let what had been building up inside of me, be delivered.

May 2018

NEXT STEP

I am nervous about seeing Kyle. Although there are many reasons feeding that nervousness, the most prominent is that our unraveling *really* hurt me. I do not want to be around Kyle because I do not want to feel the pain of that again. I want to forget the pain of that. Yet maybe it is better to feel it, to let the emotion work its way out of me.

Our relationship ended with a mutual and amicable decision. Nevertheless, I feel deeply abandoned by its ending. I keep thinking things like: Why did Kyle stop wanting what it took to make things work? When did I stop being worth it to him? Through the course of our relationship, we grew into different people with different desires. In my heart, that felt like slowly being left alone while still in a relationship. It felt like I was left with what I thought *we* wanted, holding all of our hopes and dreams by myself. I felt I could only follow Kyle into his new life if I gave up on all those things. Instead of leaving them behind, I released Kyle to pursue a new direction, as I single handedly carried all the things I thought we wanted, things that suddenly felt heavy and empty.

I am nervous about seeing Kyle because this is

another step of letting go of the need for him to love me. I mentioned to my sister how I was nervous that he might judge me. When she reminded me that it did not matter what he thought, I realized that his opinion still mattered to me because, on some level, his love must also. I recognized how a little part of me that loved him, that desperately wanted things to work out, and wanted his love back, is still alive. It is dying, but there is this stubborn little piece rolling around inside that does not quite know how to fathom or cope with what it would be like without him loving me at all. Most of the time, I do not notice it. When I do notice it, its persistent presence is painful and frustrating. I want it to be gone. Yet for some reason, I am struggling to let it go on a deep level. So, I am nervous to see Kyle because I am afraid of him not loving me anymore and finding grief and pain in that. Even more, I feel afraid of him still loving me and finding joy and comfort in that.

In the midst of trying to figure out how to process this, here is what I keep coming back to: a feeling is just a feeling. Just because I feel like I still want or need Kyle to love me, does not mean it is true. I am strong enough to see Kyle and choose the truth. I have done it before and can do it again. When I asked my mom if she thought I should go to the wedding, she told me not to give up territory to Kyle that belongs to me. That stuck.

Last night, I came home and cried and grieved,

but I also had an epiphany. As much as I feel hurt and abandoned—I have been doing hard work over the past few months, establishing my *choice* in the process. Every day I am choosing to forgive and let go of the hurt because I believe the life I already have is far better than the one I reminisce about. I am choosing to let go of the past because I believe in the future.

I believe there is someone in my future worth giving up every shred of affection for Kyle. Beyond that, I am worthy of giving up love for Kyle. I am worthy of releasing myself from the grip of his love on my life, into a more fulfilling future. To be afraid, to let myself be owned by the emotions I may feel when I see Kyle, to let myself buy into whatever story my emotions tell, is all to give up my ground. It is to give Kyle all the ground I have fought so hard to gain the past few months. No matter the feelings I feel, I will not let another person own me. I will choose to navigate my emotions with strength, bravery, and most of all, the truth of the new life I have chosen.

I think if I could relinquish the hurt, I would actually enjoy seeing Kyle. I care about him and I have missed elements of our friendship. However, what is more important than a friendship that used to be, is the call for me to guard my heart from a friendship that did not prove trustworthy of sharing my story. It is more important to guard the choices I have made: the choice not to rekindle the friendship, the choice to work toward a different future, the choice to feel grief and to move on. This work has been hard-fought, hard-earned, and precious. I must guard that from Kyle, and from a desire for his approval or the fondness of nostalgia.

In some ways, I am glad I will be seeing Kyle because I want to come out on the other side of our breakup knowing that I am brave and strong. I want to finish the business that needs to be finished to make room for what is next. I want to be soft and strong at the same time. I do not know exactly what soft and strong looks like or how to interact with Kyle. I do not want to be too hard, from a place of hurt or bitterness, because that is giving the past power over my heart. Nor do I want to be too soft and open the door for longing that will pull me back and hurt me.

Maybe longing is really why I have been so nervous. In the past, despite our relational flaws, I always loved Kyle. Being around him always filled me with a deep desire for his love. I feel afraid the residues of that are still inside and will flood my tenderly budding work. I think I am stronger now than I was in the past, but I am still questioning: how do I flood the situation with strength instead of emotion? What do I do and say?

I hold a quiet confidence that something very good will be birthed by this circumstance. Still, I feel a struggle between my old self and my new self. My old self is the one that feels abandoned, the one that cringes inside when I see friends with spouses similar to Kyle living together softly. My old self is the one who craves Kyle's love and approval. In a way, I was looking for a rescuer in Kyle and in my expectations for the love that would come after him. I think my old self wanted someone to rescue me from discontentment with my life, from feeling a deep need for help, and from doubts of my self-worth. When I think about how I felt when Kyle held me, gently touched me, or looked at me with really big eyes, it made those needs feel met in such a visceral way. Yet it also made me feel a little codependent, not as strong as I could be, and unable to be the real me for fear of losing him.

My new self is more strong and soft, willing to face challenges and willing to feel. I acknowledge that losing Kyle hurts and that I still desire a partner as some challenges are tough alone. In the same breath, I acknowledge that just because my path looks different from those around me, does not make me inferior to my peers. In some ways, this challenging path makes me feel set aside for a hard, but deep and rich, life journey. I feel this way because in these struggles, I am gifted with the opportunity to go deeper. Although it is often uncomfortable, the deeper I go, the higher the ceiling of my life expands.

My new self recognizes reality—as much as I would like to be friends with Kyle, that is not the choice that would be best and safest for my heart and story. My new self recognizes a deep need to be independent, to be able to grow and flourish, living my life without caring if he cares or knowing if he knows. Perhaps this is why I am not ready for someone else yet. Maybe this is my time for unplugging from my deep need of validation to be valid, being seen to be important, and being picked to be worthy. Maybe this is a time to grow inwardly— to grow a gentle and quiet spirit for the pleasure of no one but God and myself.

Where I have landed in all these thoughts and questions is forgiveness. How do I react to seeing Kyle? Forgiveness. Over and over and over. With every surge of desire for him to love me, with every pang of hurt over feeling abandoned, with every jaded wave of anger that inevitably comes with relational disintegration, over and over and over again, forgiveness.

With forgiveness, I release my grip on the wish that my story with Kyle would have had a different ending. Forgiveness frees me from the hurt of what happened in our story. It acknowledges emotional debts but sets both of us free as if there were none. It frees me from perpetual grief over the outcome of his love for me. Forgiveness also frees me from anger and hurt, and from carrying what was into the present. It opens my heart to acceptance, breathing, and flowing with the moment.

Most importantly, forgiveness frees me to move on. Forgiveness is mysterious in that it holds and releases at the same time. Forgiveness holds the truth of all the good things that happened. It holds all the happy memories that made me feel like I wanted to live inside of them forever. Equally, it holds the acknowledgment of all the hurt. It holds the imperfections in our dynamic and the way those impacted both Kyle and I. It holds feelings of betrayal, abandonment, and the feeling of losing my heart. Forgiveness holds all these in the light of truth, that both blends and softens these experiences. Somehow, in holding these things together, forgiveness releases them as irrelevant to my future and my happiness.

WOMB

For me, growing a new life, a new heart, a new hope, a new promise, is like growing a baby. It happens in the womb of process—a dark, silent, quiet, unseen place. For me, it happened over days and months of few people knowing my story but myself. It happened through letter writing and taking refuge in quiet moments. It happened day by day. The progress seemed imperceptible. But each day, I woke up to find that somehow, in some impossible way, the new life, the new promise, the new me, had grown and expanded a little more. I can think of no better words to end reflections on process than words I jotted down on a day when I felt a little deflated because process often felt like that—deflating, discouraging, and fruitless. The magic of the process is that it washed over discouragement and left behind something new and shimmering, like waves rinsing over sand, leaving behind beautiful shells. Although this is really more of a note than a letter, with words that seemed insignificant at the time, I see in those words a little snapshot of the overarching truth about the process. It leaves behind little treasures. You just have to have your eyes open to see them.

May 2018

PROCESS

Today, I am thankful. I am thankful for the new. I am thankful for my new haircut. I am thankful for teatime chats with my dear friend Kathleen. I am thankful for the hospitality of friends. I am thankful that when I describe the person I want to marry, I feel like that person exists. I am thankful that today's struggles birthed new inspiration for the future. This has been process.

PART IV
NEW HEART

FORWARD

O ne of the Greek words for "mind" is *phronēma*. It comes from the same root as the word diaphragm. The diaphragm, in the human body, is adjacent to one's most vital organs. It moves in harmony with the breath, which in the Scriptures, is synonymous with one's spirit. As the diaphragm synchronizes with the breath, the mind is intended to synchronize with the spirit. Your cognition and physical actions align with your visceral emotions. I think that an experience of the mind, in the truest sense, is what drives much of human ecstasy. I think it is what humans feel when they make love to someone they love, when they sing an evocative song, when they create a soulful piece of art, or when they give words to the emotional tumult inside. Mind: Inward expression becomes outward action.

I used to love Kyle in a visceral way. That was part of the agony of loving him. So often, my mind and logic did not align with my emotional experience of him. No matter where his heart was and no matter what happened between us, I was overwhelmingly in love with him. My soul ached for him. I remember the day this changed. It was a summer afternoon. We had laid by the pool together and when we returned to his apartment, a sizable disagreement emerged. After hours of exchanging words and hurts, Kyle drafted up a contract of demands I had to agree to if the relationship was to continue. He gave me a time deadline—8 pm. I panicked. I walked to the parking garage of his apartment complex and I cried, heaving big sobs. I called my mother, my mentor, my counselor, and my friend, but no one answered. I knew I should pack my bags and walk right out, but my heart was not ready to cleave in such a dramatic way. My mind and my feelings were out of sync.

In the afternoon, I was able to reach the counselor I had visited the time I took Kyle with me. He helped me loosen my grasp on some of my fears and concerns about the relationship. After the call, I reluctantly agreed to Kyle's contract and I thought that would be enough. I thought my willingness to pay for counseling, my practical demonstrations of willingness to give more in the areas he had requested, would be enough to express my commitment to Kyle. That evening, as we were walking out for dinner, he said "hey." He brought over the contract and a pen, so that I could sign before 8 pm. I gave him a blank stare. "Are you serious?" He was and I signed. But something inside of me did not feel right about it. The inward expression did not match outward action.

That night, I could not stop turning over in my heart how something about this situation felt off. Something about signing myself to contractual demands that were not mutually desired, made me feel uncomfortable. When Kyle sensed my second-guessing, he threatened to end things as he had done so many times before. I remember his heated words to me, as he ripped the contract in half, "It's over, Chelsea. We've never been able to make it work and we never will." It was too late for me to drive back to San Diego immediately, so I slept on the floor of Kyle's room. I wanted to touch him before falling asleep, just a finger on his arm, but he seemed miles away from me, as he rolled to the opposite side of his king-sized mattress. I laid awake that night, ripped through with anxiety. I laid awake, feeling the hard ground beneath me, and I prayed, wondering what to do. When morning light finally crept into the sky, I crawled up next to a still, sleeping Kyle. I snuggled close to him. As he drifted into consciousness, he rolled over and wrapped me in his arms. He placed his hands on my back and clung to me. As he held me, I asked if he would keep me. He shrugged his shoulders. When he awoke and sat up, I climbed onto his lap, wrapping my legs next to his, and placed my lips on his, face to face. I let my inner feelings flow into my outer action. But deep down there was another visceral feeling, a feeling that something was not right, a feeling that this was something I did not want to do. What I was expressing physically, I did not feel in my heart. I will never forget the pit I felt at the bottom of my stomach that morning, especially as I kissed him, even as he held me.

Something inside my heart shifted when Kyle insisted that I sign the contract. My heart retracted from him and no amount of physical affection could manufacture what was lost. I did not understand it at the time, because every breath I had drawn since meeting Kyle had been saturated with love for him. I think that is why I stayed. I was afraid that I would lose him over something temporary and foolish. What instead happened was that, as I stayed, he lost me.

I remember the last time I saw Kyle as his girlfriend. I remember driving to dinner. Over the years, Kyle and I had driven everywhere together—to weddings, to wide open fields with almost no gas, to parents' homes, and down the PCH to the beach, with the top of his Jeep open. We would saturate the drives with conversation and ample hand holding. That night, we sat in wordlessness as he blasted rap music. Over seven years, Kyle had been my best friend. No matter how similar or different our beliefs were, I could pour my heart into his with welcome reception. Over the months preceding that evening, this had changed. As we had grown apart, our holding hands and talking in the car had dissipated. I sat in the metered expletives of the music and wondered what to talk to him about. I no longer felt like I could talk to him about where my heart really was—my concerns or excitements for the future. I did not even feel like I could talk to him about God. Somewhere along the lines, the person who wanted to hear these things had disappeared. So, I made superficial conversation and wondered how I was to spend the rest of my life with this man if I did not feel comfortable talking to him about anything substantive, or if I could not bring myself to share my heart with him.

It seemed in the months leading up to this, I had lost the Kyle that I fell in love with to an identity change, to his metamorphosis into someone I did not know and could not bring myself to love, no matter how hard I tried. In truth, if I remember the situation without the emotional attachment that gripped me so strongly in those days—I think I had been losing him for a long time. For so long, he had felt like "the one" and it was hard to acknowledge the accumulation of signs that he might not be; how I was growing ever powerless in my attempts to force it. Gradual and imperceptible as they might have felt, the signs were there. There were little things—like the way I lost weight when I was with him because the anxiety of our emotional turmoil took away my appetite. Or the way he never let me touch him when we were arguing. He would withdraw his hand from mine with the cynicism that I was trying to manipulate the situation through touch, though all I wanted was to feel like we were still connected. There was the criticism of me, of my most fundamental attributes, that was neutralized with an abundance of compliments about superfluous things. There was the anxiety when he was at parties— was he doing something I would not want the future father of my children to be doing? There was life in the constant tension of never knowing if we were going to be engaged or broken up at the end of any given week, alongside the now embarrassing confession that I had to beg him more than once to stay in a relationship with me. Then there were bigger signs, like how Kyle told me the week he moved that he did not believe in the same God as he used to. We never quite recovered from that. Though once or twice he suggested we attend church to placate me, there was a way in which he talked about the beliefs most precious to me that felt derogatory and mocking, attitudes more appropriate for a partner in an intellectual dual than a life partner. There was the way that my life seemed to become smaller and smaller to revolve around him because he did not like my friends, he did not like the advice I was getting from mentors and counselors, and he did not want my family to know my location when we were together. There were dozens of women he dated every time we broke up, which made my family and friends wonder if he was using me, and if he would be faithful to me when we were married. There was the reality that his heart-melting apologies never lead to lasting change and whenever we talked about what was wrong with us, I was found solely responsible. As I sat at that stoplight with Kyle, in the silence created by the emotional separation between us, I felt the weight of all the signs and wondered if we could survive.

A week later, we broke up. A few days after the breakup, he drove to my apartment to bring me the belongings I stored at his house. I had gathered up his belongings, which I bagged with my copy of his house key, a book we had never finished, and cream for his chronically dry hands. He left without the gifts, but not before reluctantly agreeing to a conversation about what went wrong. When our conversation finished, I looked away from him, out the window, and cried. He watched me for a while and then gestured for me to come sit on his lap. I climbed on his legs and buried my tearful face into his neck and let him hold me. We talked and eventually laid down on my bed, where I held him and kissed his forehead. He pretended to not like it but looked at me with eyes full of desire, gesturing his head as he always did when he wanted me to kiss him. I refrained and shortly after, he left, still not my boyfriend.

It seems that so often our human experiences are more like my experiences with Kyle. Our minds and our emotions are wildly misaligned, creating anxiety rather than wholeness. To me, the way that my relationship with Kyle died embodies the chaos we can feel trying to unify our mind, trying to align our actions and feelings. These experiences embody the way that corporeal emotions, like love and grief, run through our actions. Sometimes, they bring healing. Other times, they bring confusion.

These letters written from the death of my relationship, illustrate my dance with the experience of the mind, my gradual surrender despite the pain and loss, to an alignment of my deepest intentions and outward actions. When I cried as Kyle watched, there was grief over the loss of him, but at a yet unrealized level, there was grief over the loss of the deep, innate love I had felt for him for so many years. I could not find it in myself anymore. As I cried, the last bit of it ran out of my soul, leaving space for my new feelings to create new actions to create new freedom. This is part of the reason why grief is so important. Grief unifies all these feelings into one visceral experience that we can step into and find healing.

I think that no book better illustrates this process than Psalms, a book of poems in the Scripture written by Israel's King David. Over and over, within the Psalms, we find this king commanding himself to praise God. Some people have taken this to mean that we are always to be happy- that we are to paste on smiles, ignoring our pain. Yet, all throughout the Scriptures, and in the Psalms especially, we see a different story. Adjacent to David's self-mandates to praise, are gory depictions of the depths of his despair. Before God, he bares the depth of his soul. He expresses anger, hatred, and a bloodthirsty desire for revenge in ways that make us shudder. It is easy to wonder how God allowed David's messy confessions to slip in the Bible. It seems more spiritual to read about a man who happily touts religious platitudes, than a man with a ravenous desire to avenge himself on his enemies. I have come to believe that these rollercoasters of emotion are in the Scriptures as instructions on how to manage our hearts and emotions.

I have learned in moments of silence and moments of weakness, learning to have a heart that is complete on its own, requires intentional care and management of its emotions. It means learning to feel, like David, letting the depths of your soul run, bleed, and pool around itself in all its gory mess. It also means stepping into the mess and taking ownership—taking ownership of what you believe, taking ownership to move towards yourself with the love, kindness, and compassion with which you want others to move toward you. You tell yourself to praise, not because you are afraid of your own feelings, but because you are engaging them. You are actively transforming your feelings into forward momentum.

In life, I have mostly experienced God meeting me on the road, exactly where I am. In becoming wild-hearted, I sometimes experienced Him asking me to meet Him where He was at. By that, I do not mean that God's presence ever left me alone in my journey. Rather, I mean that I often found God calling my heart to live at a higher level than my emotions wanted to. I think it is because He wanted to teach me a spirit of adventure, how to spiritually hike. Sometimes, the soul needs a spiritual hike, to learn the joy of running toward something it knows is true. The soul needs to discover the wonder of huffing and puffing, laboring and climbing into the unknown, to find new strength and beauty around every corner. This is what unfolds when we agree to meet God in His truth. We learn to run. We learn to feel our pain and carry it with us to higher ground.

Jesus said that the second most important thing we could do with our hearts is to love others, *as we love ourselves*. To be wild-hearted, we must love ourselves. This is not selfishness or pride or arrogance. It is a sacred agreement of the heart with what God says about us. It is taking responsibility for putting what we believe into action. It is the experience of the mind where we align our outward actions with our knowledge of the truth. It is allowing the love that we feel from God to animate our every action.

A reflection on moving through grief inevitably ends with the story of one's own heart. For me, the end product of grief, the catalyzed output of despair, hopelessness, and disappointment, was my own heart. Grief turns your heart inside out. Grief is the reverse experience of the mind. It is the experience of being overcome by instinctual emotions to such an extent that it infiltrates all of your external actions, often without alignment or agreement. Learning to grieve, to encounter and tend these emotions, turns the experience back again. Learning to grieve is simply the process of letting grief propel you toward love. Consequently, these last few letters are less and less about Kyle, and more and more about my own heart. They are the story of how I returned to the foundations of "love others as you love yourself." As I learned to romantically love Kyle less, I learned to intimately love myself more. As I uncurled him from my heart, I inevitably discovered more of myself.

These letters are a time-lapse because momentum is made up of moments. One morning you are overcome by despair. Then seemingly without anything changing, you wake up the next morning to find that something has shifted in your heart. You are a little further along the road than you were before. These letters are about how I got my mind back, the part of me that moves with breath and spirit. This is a sacred process. When your breath and your spirit, your feelings and actions, are all in alignment, dancing in mutual surrender to the wonder that each part of yourself is interdependently creating, that is WILD.

NEW TERRITORY

This is the story of how I fell in love...with Canada. Up to this point, I had never had much contact with anything Canadian, besides a small cohort of Canadian school friends and Canadian bacon. Every year around my birthday, I ask God to give me a word or a phrase that sets the tone for the upcoming year. A few nights before my first birthday following my breakup with Kyle, the phrase "New Territory" rolled into my head. At the time, I thought that this might mean a new hairstyle, new clothes, new adventures, or new places to travel.

The next day, a new thought occurred to me, "Why have I never thought about practicing in Canada before?" Previously, I assumed that I would practice medicine wherever Kyle was. When we fell apart, I thought I might move back to my hometown where I had several outstanding job offers. That day, something inside me experienced a gentle knowing that I did not want to go back to my hometown. I kept this new idea to myself. It would need to be carefully weighed with practicality and what was best for my heart. Nevertheless, I quietly explored it.

Advantageously, I had been assigned to a clinical shift with our university's only Canadian doctor. I set up a meeting with her to discuss my new idea and gain advice. After the meeting, I drove to my current host home and opened my email. In my inbox, there was coincidentally, a message from the university career department that read, "Practicing in Canada." From that point on, my life became unintentionally saturated with all things Canadian. I would buy medicines, oils, makeups, or 'fill in the blank' and find out they were coming from Canada. My classmates selected a research article for us to review as a group, and it was about research conducted in Canada. Nearly my entire clinic shift planned a trip to Canada. I tried to schedule an appointment with a friend. I could not because he was in Canada. I would browse websites, to find they were created by Canadian sources. I would pray about these things on the beach and look up to see people wearing Canadian T-shirts walking next to me as I prayed. When I processed these things with my counselor, she told me she was Canadian. One morning, while visiting my hometown, I went to church with my family. As we filed into the row of auditorium seats, my sister was greeted by an old friend, who happened to be sitting in the same row and also happened to be visiting from Canada with a group of his Canadian friends. Piling into our car after church, I noticed the license plate of the car next to us read, "Beautiful British Columbia." As we drove home, I looked out the window and noted a man bicycling peacefully, in the warm glow of the Sunday afternoon.

He wore a bright red Canadian jersey. Lounging at home that afternoon, with the members of my family each reading various articles, my mom looked up from hers and said, "Hey, do you know it's Canada Day?" Apparently!

The idea filled me with lightness, like floating on a cloud of new possibilities. The reality filled me with apprehension. Was I strong enough for this new adventure? Why was I planning to establish my life in a place where I did not know a soul? Why was I leaving warm sand and San Diego's endless summers for the cold, harsh, Canadian winters? I did not know the answers. I only knew something inside of me was being called.

Months later, I poured out these questions to my mother. We sat on a curb, waiting for movers to pack the last few bits of my furniture into the U-Haul. I ran through my list of questions, contrasted to my inability to shake Canada from my heart, to wring this mysterious country from my soul. As I rattled on, my mother, who deeply desired me to live close to home, said, "Hey look." She pointed to the side of the U-Haul. In big letters, it read, "Where will you go next? Adventure across Canada." At that moment, my affection was solidified. This country found its way into my heart before I ever found my way onto its soil.

I have come to consider Canada synonymous with my new season. Its sense of earthy nature, broad expanse, and rugged wilderness seems representative of the new chapter I feel pulled into. Slowly, life without Kyle began to piece itself back together. I woke not to a new relationship or a new change of scenery, but a broad frontier of heart and life- a wild mystery of uncharted new territory. This is the letter I wrote when that sense of newness started to take shape—my very first letter from a heart and life that no longer belonged to Kyle.

May 2018

NEW TERRITORY

This is the phrase that has been on my heart as I enter a new stage of life, start a new journal, and turn 26 years old. Struggling in this season of many transitions, moving, and not having a place to go, I have felt like something new is being born. I have known that what I felt before was labor pains, but now I feel labor.

In the background of all the things in my life that feel crushing, strangling, that I feel are pushing me beyond my breaking point—there has been music playing in my soul. I have been thinking about a song called *New Wine,*[1] about how pressing, like trodden grapes, makes wine. The "pressing" in my life makes something that, like wine, is rich and full of depth, but it makes it in my soul. All the roar and tumult of life leaves behind something that is soft, smooth, and full of power in a quiet way. In all the challenges breaking me down, breaking my heart and my strength, I am treading on new soil— covering new territory, discovering this wild freedom that pushes me even further still. I am laboring and

---

1   "New Wine" by Hillsong

laboring, and something inside of me that I never knew was there, is being born and making itself into my life. It is setting my life on fire, from new sparks that do not belong to Kyle.

Last night, something happened that expanded on this. I tried something new and felt this sense of wonder. I thought about how in the seven years Kyle had known me, I had never done this new thing. I thought, "I'm covering new territory" and at that moment, I knew that was my phrase for life's next phase: *New Territory.*

As my 26th year of life unfolds, little indications of new have presented themselves. I was promised a new place to live on my birthday. The first weekend of being 26 began with attending a wedding, a new union. I do not know exactly what God's plans are for this season. Whether new territory is something as small as new experiences, as adventurous as new places visited, or as meaningful as a new heart, I just know that this is a season for new territory.

About a year after I wrote this letter, I made it to Canada. A few weeks before my first visit, I dreamt of walking through a Canadian forest. It was snowy and cold, but I was happy. I kept running through the forest yelling "I'm free." The first time I visited Canada,

I touched down in Calgary about 2 am local time. I drove carefully on icy roads through the empty streets and could not escape the impression that Calgary was more understated than I had expected. I kept thinking that maybe Canada was not where I was supposed to end up after all. The next day, I slept in and, when I woke up, decided to go for a walk. I picked a park that I had read about online and as I was walking through it, I saw the river that was in my dream was winding its way through the center of this park.

A few months later, I visited the Canadian Rockies for a vacation. The mountains were still covered in snow and I spent most of my time hiking in this snow. On one particular hike, me and those I was traveling with drove far out on deserted roads to hike the toe of a glacier, looking for ice caves. The hiking trail was buried deep beneath feet of snow so we carefully followed footprints from other hikers, to avoid sinking or avalanche areas. The ice caves had melted before we arrived so we ended up walking in a big circle. I didn't care. When I was in Canada, I was the new person I have written about becoming all throughout this book. I was present. I was carefree. I was trying new things that I enjoyed. I kept thinking *"Kyle would have never let me do this."* And I was free.

These are the only two trips that I have ever taken to Canada. Between visa issues and unexpected pandemics, the move I dreamt of never actually took place. I don't have an answer for all the compelling indications that never came to be, but I do have peace. The dream of

Canada opened my heart to moving toward something new in practical ways. When I finished medical school, I sold all my belongings in preparation for an international move. I still drive the car I purchased to navigate harsh winters. Although I did not physically move to Canada, my dream to live there moved my heart- into a new season and into more complete realizations of the person I was always meant to be.

CASITA

I have come to learn that home is an adventure more than it is a place. So often throughout history, God's people have been wanderers. I like that, because that is what grief feels like. That is what leaving an old life and finding a new one feels like. It is not so much a mighty conquering of new territory, but a stumbling along a road that is always and only, one step ahead of you.

It is funny how afraid we are of the unknown even though it holds the future we desire. Perhaps, part of why the unknown is so terrifying is because of the way we have to dance with it. It leads. We follow. More often than not, it feels like the unknown is strangling us instead of pulling us forward. So we run instead of dance, running backward, even if what we left behind falls short of the hopes we carry for our futures.

When we move forward in our lives, we want to see a road, stretching for miles into a beautiful horizon. What I have learned is that the future prefers to unfold around us and the road is built only by our forward motion, as we take steps. The future must be built by our participation and movement. The future built by this surrender to mystery is hardly ever the future we were looking for— it is far better.

The evening before my 26th birthday, I laid awake in a panic. My mother, who had come to visit me, slept peacefully as I crept into the adjacent room to cry. We were staying in a casita (a guesthouse of sorts), in a San Diego beach town called Cardiff-By-The-Sea. It had tall ceilings with wooden beams, and copious windows that bathed the space in yellow light and ocean breeze. It was the most peaceful place I had slept in a long time. Yet, I could not sleep. I had given myself a deadline: by the beginning of June, I would have found a place to live. The beginning of June was approaching in a matter of days and I had nowhere to live. I did not even know where I would be sleeping the next week. I curled up on the casita couch and sobbed. I sobbed because I felt alone—a wandering heart without a caretaker, wildly independent with a pressing desire to be dependent. I cried because I had been turned down for a studio the size of a postage stamp that seemed like my dream; it was quiet and cheap and could have been my own. I cried because it seemed like the present was conspiring to keep me out of the future. Little did I know, I grieved my lack of a home in the very place that would become my home. The next day, on my birthday, the owner of the casita told me that he wanted to help me out. He would rent me the casita, but I had to wait until September, the end of his Airbnb season. I would wait because the casita was far beyond any home I could have dreamt for myself.

Extravagant futures are not cheap. They are bought

with risk, with waiting, with being willing to make a home of the unknown, and in my case, expensive rent. Extravagant futures, like houses, are built. They are built as we sit in the dark, engaging with our fear of tomorrow's mystery. It is here that they form, they wrap themselves around us and appear. In this way, new territory is not so much discovered as it is created. The Cardiff casita became my first real home in my new life on my own. As I waited for it, I grew a heart that could inhabit every fiber of it with life—deep and thick, and long and wide.

May 2018

WEARY

I keep thinking about the Cardiff casita and how it is a metaphor for my life right now—especially the portion of my life relating to redemption, repayment, and reconciliation of what was lost in my last relationship. A few nights ago, a thought rolled into my head as I was falling asleep. These are my favorite types of thoughts because you cannot control what you think when you are almost asleep and thoughts at this time are so rich and raw. I remember thinking, as I fluttered in and out of consciousness, that just as God was intentionally allowing a delay in my housing situation to accomplish a purpose, He was also allowing a delay in bringing me relational restoration, at least in the way I hope for it.

A few days ago, I told God that I was willing to let my grief over love lost go, but I needed Him to come through for me. I needed Him to speak a little louder, to give me a clearer direction, to tell me He had not forgotten about my desire for a relationship or my grief over lost relational pieces. I needed Him to show me who or what or when to hope for. As I prayed, I again thought of the casita. I thought of how I did not have the casita yet, but I had the tangible promise of it. I knew where it would be and what it would be. I knew the endpoint; it was just not ready yet. That is what I have been asking for in a relationship and all the things I wish to be redeemed: a vision for which I can wait and for which I can prepare.

The casita is *exactly* what I want, everything I have been hoping and looking for. Up to this point, I have said no to other living situations that became available, because I did not want to settle for something that was not quite right. Yet not settling required, and continues to require, sacrifice. An exact match for what I wanted has come but it requires me to sit in a place that I do not want to be in, longer than I want to. I feel it is the same in looking for a life partner. If I do not settle, what I am looking for will come. Yet, it is going to take me being in a place I do not want to be, a place of interim and transition, longer than I want to be.

This weekend, I attended a wedding and it caused me to realize that there are relational hopes which I have given up. I believe that God wants to restore more than the fullness of what I lost. He wants to give back to me what I lost with Kyle and then some—something healthier and purer, safer and softer. This has seemed impossible and far away. So, I have poured my heart into the emotional change in front of me, forgetting about the precious things I loved in the past: the things that made me stay, the things so rare that I did not know if I would find them again. In my exhaustion, I forgot those things could exist and how I was allowed to hope for them. Instead of hope, I have felt at my breaking point. I have been striving so hard with every piece of my heart in every aspect of life, and it seems in vain. My life looks unchanged and unmoved, like one big heap of rubble, that is too much for me to clear. Despite my best efforts at belief, my life feels like one shattered heart that needs healing. Today, I told God that I give up. I do not have the energy margin for happiness right now. After I prayed that, I read this Scripture that a friend had shared with me, "Let us not become weary in doing good, for at the proper time we will reap a harvest if we do not give up."[1]

These words created such a poignant contrast to my exhaustion and my decision to give up. The phrase "Do not become weary" stood out to me. I pondered how in showing me that the home and the heart I long for are still a little ways off, God was also showing me that I am going to need a second wind to make it to the end. Somehow, the second

---

[1]   Galatians 6:9 New International Version

wind I need is one born from my surrender into the rest and enjoyment of God, a laying down of my persistent attempts to try to chisel out the future I think I need from the life in front of me now.

I have been reminded of how in the Scriptures, wind often symbolizes God's Spirit. There is something mystical and catalytic that happens when God's Spirit blows across a situation. Everything changes but from a place of ease and not a place of striving. Just as my Cardiff casita appeared in the very spot where my own effort fell short, I feel God is showing me that my second wind and my second life are not dependent on me. He will send me a second wind of His strength, His rest, His joy, to help carry me to the things I long for, things that are still a long way off. Rest in the midst of such a pressing shift calls me to surrender to that terrifying unknown, to step forward in trust that home can be found in this uncertain place. This gentle movement of the heart, this dance, is a creative process. Here, releasing is creating. The process brings Spirit into struggle, bringing rest from wrestling, wine from breaking, home from wandering, future from wondering.

FINDING ME

Our mutual friends were married the first weekend of June. I think my life changed that weekend, actually my whole story changed that weekend. I had prepared myself for two circumstances. The first was that Kyle would bring his girlfriend and I would have to process the pain of watching him love someone else. The second was that Kyle would not bring his girlfriend and I would feel his gentle, constant love for me, beneath carefully placed words and stolen glances. This had happened once before.

A few years prior, Kyle and I happened to be at a recital for the groom. Kyle had a girlfriend at the time, so we were careful with each other—talking, but not too much, being polite but not affectionate. Through our silent interactions, we both internally resolved that we loved each other. I drove away that night, with a horrible feeling in the pit of my stomach, afraid I would never see Kyle again. Being around him was like magic. It stirred up something deep and powerful that I had not known was still there. I knew that I knew, deep in my core, my heart, and my bones, that this was the man I wanted to love for the rest of my life. He knew the same about me and the next time I saw him, he did not have a girlfriend.

That is not what happened at the wedding. What happened was a scenario I was totally unprepared for. I could tell you the story of the grin he flashed when I walked in, of how I wondered if he was sneaking looks at me during the toasts, of how we smiled at each other when he walked over to help light my sparkler, or of the jokes he sprinkled into my conversation with a friend standing near him. However, those moments are not what colored the evening for me. Those are a collection of moments that are a stretch at best. What I felt was the complete absence of conversation between us, and the fact that he appeared to walk out of his way to avoid talking to me. What I felt was him answering me with thumbs up, when I asked him how he was doing. Such a sharp contrast to planning our own wedding at the same time last year. I felt the sting, the rejection, the sadness, the heaviness, the numbness, the hollowness of the shell of a love that was now gone.

After the wedding was over, I called his sister and processed my hurt with her. A few days later, I received an invitation from a friend to go to Japan. As life went on and plans were made, the pain was anesthetized day by day. I had people to talk to and things to look forward to—my head was above water until one afternoon when I received a text. It was from the friend I had arranged to stay with over the summer until the casita was ready. She explained she would not be able to host me as anticipated.

With no idea where I would be living in a few weeks and physical exhaustion racking my bones, I had to turn down the trip to Japan. When this transpired, I snapped. The dull, aching levy of sadness in my heart broke, overflowing into an all-consuming, overwhelming abyss. It felt like a bottomless pit I had not known existed. That day, I went to bed and cried like I never have before. Lying on the air mattress of my friend's guest bedroom, sandwiched between her desk and her boyfriend's music equipment, I cried all day long, mourning the most painful grief of the breakup I had yet endured. I cried and wrote, letting the deep darkness simmer to the surface of my cognizance. This day changed my life.

Though I had said many times I was choosing to let Kyle go, deep down I clung to the belief that he would continue loving me even after we were broken up, as he always had before. The wedding revealed to me that this was not true. I found myself being reborn into a new world in which saying I was okay without someone romantically loving me was no longer an emotional exercise—but a reality I was forced to confront. Although a new life is what you are supposed to find after grief, this reality felt like a life I did not want. Though I had tried to let go of Kyle, I was totally unprepared for Kyle letting go of me. His release made me feel shell shocked—unsure how to navigate a world in which Kyle did not love me.

Through sobs and sobs of heart-crushing emotion, I felt. I *felt*, for the first time, that this was no longer my story with Kyle. That had ended long ago. For better or worse, this was *my* story. As I wrote, I learned to re-write. I learned to take ownership of that new story. I found under what felt like the end, under soul-piercing sadness, under not knowing how to begin, was my heart. It was waiting for me to see it, notice it, love it, and free it into a brand-new life of its own.

June 2018

BROKEN

I think I have figured it out this exhaustion I have felt. This week, I popped. For a long time, I held an optimism that things would shift, that something in my life would burst. But this week, I felt stuck and burned out, as everything I tried to create that shift failed. Today, I feel like my life is in a million broken pieces and despite my best efforts, I do not know how to put it back together.

This week, I am recognizing that I made Kyle my source of love. Together or apart, I was okay because he loved me. I had worth because someone could not get over me. When I saw him this weekend, it was different. He showed every indication of being over me and I spiraled. I see now that I have not been able to cope with the pain of being someone he rejects. So instead, I have been trying to become someone he regrets.

I have been trying to be more beautiful, working tirelessly to perfect my hair, skin and fitness, trying to be worthy of his love. I have been trying to be more exciting, desperately planning travel, looking for things to make me more adventurous. I have been trying to be more successful, looking for ways to prove I can achieve and make money without him. The sum of my efforts is that I have been trying to be a perfectly beautiful, super fit, nomadic adventurer (aka homeless), world traveler, real estate investor, youth volunteer, social butterfly, medical student—all while also balancing my health issues. That is what I thought I needed to be to keep a partner loving me.

After the wedding, I kept thinking of things that would have helped Kyle love me. Maybe if I would have talked to him at the wedding, he would have wanted to talk to me. Maybe if I would have been more gracious about the things I did not like in a relationship, he would have wanted to keep trying. Maybe if I would have been more available to travel, or maybe if I would have taken him to the shops near my house, I would have been entertaining enough for him. I would have been enough for him. Since we broke up, I have not only been trying, I have been running—running from every piece of me that I felt was not good enough for Kyle, which is pretty much all of me. I have had this desperate need to feel new and I think this need comes from the fact that I have been rejecting myself because Kyle did not love me. No wonder I am so tired.

Now, I cannot go to Japan and I feel worthless. My house plans fell apart and I feel like a failure.

My spirit says, "be unseen." This is hard for me. My whole life, I have felt passed over and unloved. Even now, I feel I do not possess enough worth to keep a partner engaged in loving me, but I am too tired to keep trying. My whole body hurts. In giving up trying, I am left with all the parts of me that were unacceptable to Kyle. I am left with these parts of myself to love, take care of, and cherish.

I do not know how to start, and I feel a lot of shame; shame that I made Kyle my love source, shame that I do not know how to start over, shame that I have been trying to advertise my worthiness and shame that I do not want to stop doing that. The only starting point I see is a willingness to be unloved in the way I want to be loved: a willingness to be unseen. I do not know how to sit in these depths.

It feels like I have work to do. I think I started feeling abandoned a long time ago before I ever met Kyle. I felt abandoned by God, to a man who hurt me, and to compensate I decided to make men my love source from then on out. If they accepted me, approved of me, and wanted me, I thought that was love.

Beyond learning to unplug from that, part of the work of this moment also means acknowledging the reality of the pain it presents. It is a painful thing to completely give your heart to someone and have them reject you in any capacity. I am learning to deal with and swallow that. It is hard to give your whole self to someone, to take off all the armor for them, and have them say no. It reminds me of a letter I wrote to Kyle when we were broken up years ago. I read it to him when we got back together the final time. It was about all the ways his love had changed me, softened me, and helped me grow. It was about all the ways we were different and how perfectly complementary each was, and how we needed each other. The words of this letter remind me how I let Kyle in as I had never let anyone else in before. I let him see my need for him, my deep desire for him to accept me.

I have been thinking about some happy memories we had together at this time last year. This time last year was mostly joyful, we were closer than ever, just starting to fray but caught up in the love bubble and planning our lives together. I remember one particular day at the beach. We had been laying in the sand and running around in the water together. As we were playing in the waves, we were talking about when Kyle was going to propose. He had his arms wrapped around me, and he told me he was afraid that I would get tired of living with him after we married. I told him that I would never get tired of him and I would always want him—and I meant it. That was part of the wonder of Kyle. Someone I wanted, wanted me back. Someone I needed, needed me back. The person I loved with all my heart, loved me more. And he did not just love me—he saw me, understood me, and made me more me. It is like the minute Kyle laid eyes on me, he pierced straight through to my soul and wanted me even more because of it. His relentless pursuit of who I was inside, filled me with a sense of value I had never experienced before; it made me more alive. But in the end, he found me unacceptable.

Being rejected by Kyle is like no rejection I have faced before. The ones in the past, while temporarily painful, were not vulnerable. I was rejected by people whose love I did not need, who were not that invested, and who I could easily forget. I was rejected by people who had not made it very close to my heart. Kyle was different. He completely infiltrated my heart and soul, and his heart beat with mine. My whole life was planned around my need for his love and although we both chose to end things, I felt like he left me alone to pick up the pieces. So my life feels new, but in the worst way, totally broken and confusing. The scariest part of this whole new season is being stripped down to just me without any bells and whistles. It is scary because it makes me wonder who will love me, if anyone will love me. It places me in a position of terrible vulnerability. Here I am with nothing to offer and someone might say no. They might do to me again what Kyle did, what my childhood friends did, and what I have done to myself.

I have spent my whole life running from who I am, trying to run into what would make me feel a sense of worthiness. In light of that, I have had this paradoxical wonder—what if all the bells and whistles I look to to give my life value, are what is keeping me from drawing in the love I desire? It reminds me of this verse in the Bible, "If I speak in the tongues of men and of angels but have not love, I am only a resounding gong or a clanging cymbal."[1] Without love for God, for others, and for myself at the core of all those bells and whistles, they become unattractive noise. They become diversions, smokescreens for love, which is often much more raw and unrefined than all my smooth, shiny bells and whistles.

I think of the good ways in which I experienced Kyle loving me, the moments of feeling cherished and pursued, of opening myself to trust and vulnerability because of that pursuit. I am starting to realize that is how I am supposed to experience God loving me. As I go through this process, I am reminded of a poem I have turned over and over in my heart this year. It is the one I stumbled across on Valentine's Day,—the one about fires and cities, and learning to find love independent of another human being. Ever since I read this poem I loved it, because God had been speaking to me about setting the past and the present on fire, and a thought occurred to me that perhaps love could do that. Setting the past on fire meant doing away with ties to an expired future, but setting the present on fire

---

1   1 Corinthians 13:1 New International Version

meant a wholehearted pursuit of what makes me come alive. I am marveling because, as I learn to love myself as God loves me, it is incinerating my need for the feeble love substitute of the past. This love is burning away the need for all the accomplishments and accouterments I thought I needed to be valuable. Beneath all that, I am discovering a vibrant joy for who I am that illuminates my present and keeps me roaring towards tomorrow. I see exactly what that poem describes unfolding in my heart. And I am coming alive.

FREE FALL

I f I am being perfectly honest, sometimes it feels like faith fails. We have high hopes, deep dreams, and broad faith for genuinely good requests, but sometimes those things turn out much differently than we expect or ask them to. Dreams fall apart. Prayers seem unanswered. Hope feels disappointed.

As I have fallen more in love with Canada, I have noticed something about Canadians. I feel like beneath their national identity is a sacred kinship to the great beyond, a respectful exploration of the great unknown that is approached in wonder instead of conquest. I want that. I want to suck the marrow out of life. I want to be adventurous, spontaneous, seizing every opportunity, running into the great unknown with open arms.

I have learned that if you live this way, you will fail. You will extend yourself to people and they will reject you. They will be uninterested or misjudge your motives. You will grow dreams and pursue hopes that will fall apart. Yet, if you keep living this way, it will lead you to the people who will say yes, the one in a million dreams that were worth all the nos. To live in a way that is wild-hearted requires risk. It requires intimacy with the unknown and resiliency to failure.

When Kyle and I first broke up, I took the approach of conquering the unknown. I wanted to plan my life: when my next relationship would be, where I would live next, and what color my future children's eyes would be. I would pray about each item to make sure I got it "right." It seemed like I was planning an adventure, but I was really constructing a bondage. I was trying to bend and shape something untamable, the great beyond, into little boxes that would keep me from getting hurt again. What I found is that love does not exist in algorithms or plans. It exists in uncertainty and risk.

Recently I watched a movie about Alex Honnold, the free solo rock climber who scaled El Capitan without ropes. There is a part in the movie where neuro-imaging reveals that his amygdala, the part of the brain responsible for emotion, dramatically under-functions. The image technician explains the practical implications of this: the experiences that elicit emotion in most people do not have the same effect on him. He requires much greater stimuli, like climbing a mountain where one faulty step could lead to his death, to evoke emotional activity in his brain. I was captivated by that because I saw his climb playing out a human truth that most of us experience in a microscopic way in our own hearts. Of course his climb played it out on a much grander, riskier, more magnificent scale, but it invoked inspiration just the same. During his practice climb, he memorized the rock while wearing ropes and he fell a few times along the way. As I watched, I wondered if there was something about the risk of removing the ropes and its demand for everything inside of him that actually changed his body's physiology to give him what he needed to succeed.

As I watched his accomplishment, it inspired me in a new way. I do not want to climb rocks, but I do want to love the same way he climbed—without strings or restraints and in a way that demands everything inside of me. I want to love in such a way that if my love fails, I will most certainly be hurt and shattered. If I have learned one thing from loving until I broke, it is that love is worth the heartbreak. Despite all of the pain I felt in losing Kyle, I would risk being hurt again for love. I may love more wisely or more healthily in the future, but I would undoubtedly fiercely and bravely love another again because I believe there are people in life worth loving like that. I believe that life itself is worth loving like that.

In the movie, Alex's mother said that free soloing and climbing without ropes is what makes her son feel most alive. As I slowly unraveled the illusions that made me feel safe in my life, I discovered that only in loving with consequence could I feel alive.

June 2018

FEAR OF DOING THINGS WRONG

I have a fear of doing things wrong. In this whole process of dreaming up a new life, I have struggled to relinquish the idea that things may not turn out exactly as I hope or imagine or even pray. To me, this means that sometimes I may hear God incorrectly, an idea I have been terrified to explore.

Maybe I have been using this fear of getting things wrong as a way to self-protect. If I hear God "correctly" every time, if there is a map for my life, that means there is the comfort and joy of what I hope for *certainly* happening. It means I know how things end and it is nice and predictable. It means not totally facing the emptiness of letting go.

If I am wrong sometimes, that means I have to face some difficult things. It means a great big question mark. It means sitting in discontent and the unknown. It means I sometimes see things in people that they do not see in me. It means extending myself and not always being appreciated. Yet, it also means that I can blame the unknown on myself. When life is confusing and not going the way I hoped, when the future is uncertain, when the present is broken—I can blame it on myself. I can analyze what went wrong and I can do better next time to protect myself from getting hurt again. If it is *my fault* when things fall apart—some faulty footing on the path of life, some negligence in hearing what God really wanted to say, then life is never beyond my control.

I do not want to hold my future hopes too closely because I think God wants me to face the emptiness of letting go, releasing that false sense of control. It stings but I hear something brave and resilient inside me whispering, *"So what? So what if your hopes come to nothing and your dreams die again? These are feelings you will have to face a lot in life. Your own dreams are not where your hope lies. Your dead dreams are not the end of your story."*

Conversely, I do not want to hold too tightly to the idea that my hopes and dreams are inevitably wrong because I do not want to control my way out of uncertainty. I do not want to prematurely label them as "incorrect" because I cannot sit under the weight of "wait and see". I think the answer is somewhere in between these two states of being.

Maybe the things that have happened this past year were not so much about me hearing right or wrong. Maybe I just heard something beyond my understanding. Maybe I heard right, and the outcome was different for a reason I do not understand. I am learning to give God my fear of the unknown, with the acknowledgment that it is not actually helping protect me from future hurts. That same brave little voice inside me is asking, *"What if I was made for this?"* What if I was made not to conquer or control or run from the unknown but instead, to cultivate it? What if this place from which we run, is the place where God's people demonstrate they are His people by flourishing and growing, and even resting?

I still have a lot of discovery to do in this area. How is God protecting me? How do I allow myself to go into the fear and drive it out with truth and love? I do not know, but I do know that as I begin to relinquish fear of doing things wrong, I am free falling. And God, I want to let go.

I am not saying that getting over heartbreak is in any way comparable to the achievement of a daring free solo rock climb. At the same time, I believe that part of what makes grand human achievements so grand is the fact that, although I may never accomplish them, I can relate to them. As I let go of figuring things out and let myself fall into the unplanned, uncharted, and unknown, I found that Jesus, the Rock I had always clung to, was still there. He was there with all the crevices and crannies of safety and goodness that I had known to be true with or without the constructs I attached to Him to make me feel safe. He was the same. Nothing had changed except the fact that I was less afraid and more alive.

NOURISH YOUR DREAMS

I remember how Kyle sparked inside of me the desire to have children. He made me want to be a mother. I had always known I eventually wanted to be a mother, but not in an instinctual way. I was not like some girls who prepared for motherhood the moment they hit puberty. When my health worsened, I kind of forgot about the desire to have children altogether. Yet there was something about Kyle that brought those dreams to life in me. His big blue eyes colored them. Suddenly, I dreamt of being a wife and a mother, because I could not think of any more intimate way to nurture this man that I loved. There was something so tender about the thought of growing his children inside of my body and then spending my life putting my heart and his heart inside of theirs. I wanted to be a wife and mother because I wanted to be his wife and the mother of his children. When my relationship with him died, it felt like those dreams died too. They became stale, silent, and forgotten.

Perhaps one of the most difficult parts of the grieving process comes after it stops being so acute. When grief stops screaming in your ears, drowning your heart with every inhale, there comes this deep, eerie silence, which is terrifying in its emptiness. The silence is the stage in your life when the storm has passed but the morning has not yet broken. All you have to sustain you are promises that your dreams will live again. In this space, those promises can come to look more like shadows, shifty and uncertain. The uncertainty creates a chasm in your heart- a space that is not the future, not the past, and most certainly not whole.

You can escape the silence if you try. You can fill it with activities, parties, new relationships, travel, or plans for a new life. But my prayer is that everyone who grieves feels the silence. I hope that in its season, you allow yourself to feel the emptiness of waking to no one beside you, without arms around you, of no voice delighting to hear yours, of no belly carrying children, of no ring around your finger. Because in this silence a type of certainty grows. A certainty about yourself grows—a deep, steady knowing of who you are, despite what tomorrow brings. In the silence, you learn to grow something from nothing, like pregnancy and motherhood.

I wrote this letter during a particularly silent week, while staying alone at the home of a friend who was on vacation. It was not until life became silent that I could actually hear. The swirling grief, doubt, hope, and anxiety inside of me became still and I realized that all the dreams I felt like I had lost, were still alive in a different way.

June 2018

LOST DREAMS

In the last few days, I have been insatiably hungry. Last night I was unable to sleep and, despite all I had eaten earlier in the day, I felt this aching hunger. I mentioned it to my mom today, and she said, "I wonder if it's something spiritual."

The other day, during counseling, Sarah and I conversed about a grounding, rooting feminine energy. Our conversation provoked me to think about the Hebrew concept of mother. The Hebrew term for mother is *chavah em kol chai.* It means "mother of all living" and is derived from a Hebrew word meaning "living one." It is a self-existent and generative word, representing the very essence of life and the way that life shares itself with others through its innate creativity and self-expression. The term "mother of all living" embodies the ability to nourish and enhance all aspects of life, to see potential and develop it.

I have always loved this, because the biblical introduction of a woman[1] being called mother occurs immediately after (and almost as a response) to a story which has been distorted to blame women for all the brokenness in the world. In reality, this story honors and elevates women, even after mistakes. Instead of blaming them for all that is fractured

---

1   Genesis 3:20

in the world, it calls them out as strong healers of that brokenness. In this story, the woman is honored not just by God, but also by the man who initiated blaming her, as he bestows her with the title of mother, of *Chavah:* someone who can call life and order out of the death and chaos that has just entered the world.

I also love this story because the woman is called mother before conceiving any children. When I was fifteen, I was diagnosed with a condition that doctors said would likely make me infertile. Since that diagnosis, I have experienced many years in which my entire life felt barren. So, I love this concept and story— it is a statement about the identity of a woman. It is a declaration that a mothering spirit is intrinsic to what it means to be female. It is a picture that to be a woman means carrying life within you and nurturing it around you, affecting change through kindness, and using your voice to call out the good in others. It means that even in the barren seasons, life is still developing inside and through me.

I thought about this as I left my appointment with Sarah. I saw a mental picture of myself pregnant and heard the word "nurture" impressed very strongly on my heart. Quickly, this word expanded to the phrase "nurture your dreams." As I was lying in bed, hungry and unable to sleep, I thought about this tension I have felt of late. There are some dreams I feel God Himself has implanted into my heart that He is now asking me to lay down. Yet, I have struggled to loosen my grip, because I desire those dreams so badly. I have been wrestling with this in my spirit—is it possible to hope and release at the same time? If I have hope in my heart, am I truly laying down in my heart?

As I lay in bed, I asked myself: who gave me these dreams? Where did they originate? In the quiet of the night, I acknowledged that I truly believe these new hopes are God inspired. This is scary to acknowledge because of the possibility that I am wrong. There is the possibility that these dreams are nothing more than silly flights of my imagination that will lead me to getting hurt again. Yet, I cannot shake the sound of God's voice whispering into these dreams over and over again "get your hopes up." Herein lies the tension—finding the bravery to name my desires, to believe I can have desires that are from God, asking and hoping for those desires, while laying them down in the vulnerability of knowing that I may not have the vision for them exactly "right." It is easier to forget them entirely, to write them off as insignificant, incorrect, or imagined. But maybe, I need to be brave enough to risk being wrong or disappointed, instead of letting fear keep me enslaved to an emotionally captive state of existence. Perhaps this is the most honest thing I can do.

This reminds me of a dream I had a few nights ago. In the dream, God told me to make a list of the five things bringing me the most comfort right now and to give them to Him. In this directive, there was a sense that it was not about losing these things, but rather about releasing them to be developed and purified. When I woke from this dream, a new thought occurred to me. Maybe God not giving me things I am asking for does not mean He is saying no. Maybe the delay, the asking me to release into the unknown, is the demonstration of His grace. It is the reminder that He wants me to possess these things fully, from a wholehearted and healed place.

Today, I listened to a message about relating to God as children rather than as slaves or orphans. The speaker mentioned that you know you are relating to God like a slave if you are stuck in religion, performance, and trying to please God by getting things right. That sounded a lot like me—obsessed with getting my dreams "right," handling them the "right" way so I do not get hurt again. The speaker also said that you know you are relating to God like an orphan if you never ask for anything or if you ask for scraps without expecting great things. That sounded like me too—afraid to believe that my dreams might actually be from God. He explained that God wants to give us good things, but will wait until we are spiritually mature enough to receive them in their fullness. He wants us to receive His blessings from a place of true identity, as children of God, not as slaves or orphans. Yet, our spiritual maturity is the product of our identity and our truest identity is formed only when we can plug into God as our source of love.

Suddenly, I understood why it is not yet time for me to possess some of the good things God desires to give me. I am still learning to live as whole and loved and to love myself. While this will be a lifelong journey (one that I will never truly complete on this side of life), I have spent so many years searching for my identity in Kyle's love, and then in the love of whoever is coming next, that I am still unlearning this. If I was given what I hoped for now, I would break it or it would break me, because I would simply plug a self-loathing, broken self into another love source that falls short of the fullest love source God has for me —Himself.

I think Jesus described this dynamic perfectly when He said "And no one puts new wine into old wineskins. If he does, the wine will burst the skins— and the wine is destroyed, and so are the skins. But new wine is for fresh wineskins."[2] Likewise, a new love and a new future cannot be sustained in the same broken patterns of my old self.

The speaker in my message also described this concept pretty well. He said that people who are disconnected from knowing themselves perpetuate cycles of fear in their own lives—they are afraid of being unknown and unloved by others, but also of being known and rejected by others. This has been my life. That has been my fear and that is

---

2   Mark 2:22 English Standard Version

the narrative I played out with Kyle. I am beginning to see that this fear comes from a lack of knowing who I am.

Brené Brown says that people who feel loveable are the ones who simply believe that they are worthy of love and connection. She compares this confidence in one's own worth to the Northern Star, the light that guides us on our journeys. In my journey, I have been relating to God like an orphan and a slave—that I have to get it right or I am going to be hurt and miss the blessings. At the end of the day, I have not believed that God actually wants to give me blessings. What does God say about Himself? He says that He is love and love does not insist on its own way. God wants a parental and partnered process, rather than a perfect process. He wants a process where my desires matter, where He reveals things to me, and allows me to figure things out in the safety of His grace.

So maybe, this act of laying down my dreams is not about whether they are right or wrong, not about stripping myself of them by force. Rather, it is an act of nurturing them—that by holding my dreams in this state of stillness and apparent limbo, I am pouring love on them, allowing them and myself to grow and develop into what they need to become. Maybe I am carrying life in me until it is ready to be delivered. Yet nurturing while waiting, takes input and intention to sustain. Maybe that is why I have been so hungry, because my body knows what my soul is still discovering. As I lay in bed last night, hungry and pondering, lyrics from a song I almost never listen to crept into my head.

It is a song about the way that feelings grow. They start small and quiet, like a whisper or impression and they grow. They grow into hopes, into words, into thoughts and eventually become war cries that drive our lives forward. Sometimes, as life changes, it feels like we are forgetting these hopes and dreams. Sometimes, they are just a small feeling in the quiet of our own hearts—one that no one else feels, sees, or believes. They are feelings we think that perhaps we should forget too. Yet, shift and change do not mean goodbye. Our feelings will grow again. They will become dreams again. They will become the cries that drive us forward in our pursuits of light. As we follow light in the dark of our journeys, like the Northern Star in the night sky, our dreams will call us back when it is time. When they are ready to be delivered.

ORDINARY IS SACRED

Today, I walked on my favorite beach. There has always been a sense of restfulness to this beach. It is lined on one side by charming houses with wooden shingles and big windows. On the other side, is the smooth sand, with the water lapping up onto it. Across the street from the beach is a darling yellow house, with red flowers under the window and sometimes, a black sports car parked on the street in front of it. I once sent a picture of that house to Kyle, telling him I had found our future house. Flowers for me, a convertible for him, and a beach for us.

Today, I walked on that beach and for some strange reason, remembered the time I brought him there. It was the time we laid next to each other in the warm sand and played in the water—the time I told him I would always love him. While we were there, I found a sand dollar. I had always wanted a sand dollar. Kyle gestured to it and said, "Chelsea, wait!" Thinking he was going to tell me I should not take it home, I snatched it away from him and it crumbled into a handful of broken pieces. Kyle looked at me and said, "I was going to tell you to be careful. It's fragile."

Today, as I walked on the beach, I remembered that part of our beach trip for the first time in a long time. And, as I walked along the beach, I found another sand dollar. It is the first sand dollar I have found since that day on the beach with Kyle, although I have wanted another one since the instant the first one had broken. I picked this one up, polished it with my fingertip, and carried it home very gently. I held it flat in my hand and admired it, brushing off the sand as if I were cleaning a diamond. There was something very sacred about that sand dollar. What were the chances of finding one on the exact same beach on the exact same day I remembered finding the old one? It felt like a promise: the promise of a new life, of new treasures to be found—treasures I have forgotten I even wanted. Tonight, I carried that little sand dollar with great gentleness to a shelf in my bathroom. Then, I stood on my front doorstep and watched the patch of sky above my fence turn a brilliant pink.

This letter is not at all about Kyle. It is about how I emerged to the new life, feeling fresh and fragile, like the sand dollar I pulled from the ocean waves. To truly inhabit a new life, you have to inhabit the individual moments that lead to that new life. You have to develop eyes to see hidden gems, like that little shell, hiding in the sand. You have to breathe into every moment—the good, bad, and the ugly. If you do, you will find beauty. You will watch the sky of your life change colors, lighting itself in brilliance. This is a letter I wrote that captured how I did that. I wrote it from one of the last homes I stayed in before moving into the casita. I hated that home. It was dark, far from school, made me feel sick, and the neighbor looked at me like he was undressing me whenever I walked in and out. In that place, I had to inspect life very closely for hidden treasures. Like any kind of darkness, it somehow made life more beautiful because it brought the tiny things to life. And I felt thankful, for the skin on my bones and the brand-new skin on my heart.

July 2018

ORDINARY AND HOLY

Tonight, as I write, I can look through the frame of the one small window in my bedroom and see signs for 7/11, Shell, McDonald's, Chipotle, Costco, and CVS—a neon kaleidoscope. My window is open because it was 105 degrees today and my air conditioning is broken. Through it, I can hear nearby industrial fans rumbling, sirens whining their way through the darkness, and the bustle of cars on the highway. There seems to be nothing holy about this particular moment.

I went to the mall alone last weekend. This is something I never would have done before. I would have felt weird or lonely, like a conspicuously homeless heart. However, this outdoor mall offered a respite from my dark room, a chance to walk around under open sky, warm sun, and coastal breezes. So I hopped into my car and headed to Pressed Juicery, which serves the healthy version of mall ice cream. Here too, I did something a little outside my ordinary. I paid extra for toppings.

I sat in the sun eating my frozen treat, to the background hustle that was strangely meditative. As I looked down at the toppings, the raspberries and almond butter nestled like little treasures in the slopes and swirls of the frozen juice, I thought about how I was glad my parents had not always been able to afford things like ice cream toppings, when I was a child. I learned to appreciate the value of a raspberry instead of expecting it. Learning to be satisfied with less taught me to delight more deeply in small things. I wondered if, as a parent with the financial ability to buy ice cream toppings for my children, I will always say yes. When I become a parent, I want my children to learn to value small things so that they can more fully enjoy life. That prompted me to think about God's no—God, who has all love in His heart for His children and God who has all the resources with which to lavish on us all that we desire. I wondered if He sometimes says no to things He can afford to help us grow into a fuller life. Suddenly, I realized that right there at the mall, surrounded by noise and crowds, God was speaking to me.

When I finished the ice cream, I got up and walked around. For the sake of enjoying the time, I stopped in a few shops. In one, I came across a romper that was unlike anything I would usually choose, but I felt this strange pull to try it on. I took it down from the rack and put it back. I fiddled with the price tag, which even at 40% off, was still hefty. I took it down again. As I looked at it, it reminded me of a dress my grandma kept at her house for me, when I was a child. The dress was white and embroidered with colorful chickens. I loved that dress and always asked to wear it when I visited her house. To this day, there is still a picture in her bedroom of me wearing that dress. It reminds me of the joy I experienced as a child. I put the romper back, visited a few other shops, and left empty-handed.

I have not known what to buy lately, because I have not felt very sure of what I really like. As I shopped, I realized that for many years, I dressed to nurture my inner child, since that was the part of myself that needed healing. I liked everything frilly, innocent, and adorable. For some time after that, I dressed to nurture who I thought I should have been when I met Kyle because that was the part of myself that needed healing. I gravitated toward crop tops and short shorts. Over time, my closet grew to be a reflection of myself—a hodge-podge mess of hand me downs and mixed identities. With this move, I have been cleaning things out, throwing away what is old and worn out, and what I do not like. I am learning to be very careful before making any purchases because I want to make sure to buy things that I love, the things that reflect who I am now, because while I am still incomplete—I am whole.

I walked away from that mall empty-handed but wholehearted. And I thought of something that

God laid on my heart that morning. "Everything is sacred." I am not saying this means that evil is sacred, but that every moment of my life that is inhabited with breath, is inhabited with the sacredness of God's presence. When He is there, every moment, every ordinary experience, is sacred. I learned that last weekend, as my errand for ice cream became a time for my soul to be nourished and changed. The same is true about my life right now. Every moment of transition, change, and unglamorous mundane is holy catalytic ground.

Today, I laid on the floor of this room, and for the first time since living here, I realized there are trees outside that one small window—trees moving gently and growing quietly, toward an open sky.

KEEPING
TENDERNESS ALIVE

yle taught me how to kiss with my eyes closed.
When we first started, I kissed mostly with my
eyes open. It made me feel safe and secure,
aware of my surroundings, like if anyone walked in on
us, I would not be caught with my tongue down his
throat. Kyle hated it. Sometimes, I would kiss him with
my eyes closed and, just for a moment, flutter my lids
open to scan over his shoulder. "Close your eyes," he
would say, without even opening his. He could feel it.
Because kissing with my eyes open was actually about
kissing with my heart closed. There was a vulnerability,
a tenderness, I was afraid of opening up to. I was afraid
of letting my heart free fall into his. But I did learn to
kiss with my eyes closed. Likewise, I learned how to
love and receive love tenderly, to present my heart so
soft to another person, that he could break it with the
blink of an eye.

In the first stages of grief, all I could remember was
tenderness. In the gaping absence of a heart withdrawn

from mine, all I could remember were the moments that defined the sweetness of its presence. I remembered the way his eyes would get twice as big when looking at me, and the times he shed tears over how deeply he felt for me. I remembered the way he used to wrap his arms around my waist or touch the small of my back throughout the day, a gentle reminder that he was thinking of me and he loved me, even as I washed dishes or deliberated over kombucha flavors at the grocery store. I remembered the times we drove all night to see each other and how we looked at each other sleepily, under the moonlight, when we were finally together. I remembered the surge of life I felt the first time our hands touched, the shy way I first laid my head on his shoulder, the time we discovered we shared the same favorite part of a kiss, the time he was angry and I asked him to hold me. I remembered how when he held me, he whispered into the dark "I want to spend a long time with you, Chelsea." I remembered moments so sweet and so deep, writing them would make my heart ache.

Eventually, the aching turned to anger, and I remembered something entirely different. I remembered all the reasons we were not together. I remembered all the things that made me fall out of love. I remembered the times he told me he would not love me if I got fat, and when he told me if I was non-compliant with his requests, he could find plenty of other girls who wanted to date him. I remembered how I never knew if he was about to break up with me or propose to me. I remembered all our disagreements and how my blood boiled inside when I thought of them. I remembered the way the people who loved me cringed when they heard how he treated me.

Next, came the aching of another kind. I remembered my mistakes with Kyle. I remembered how the relationship ended. I have written about little pieces of it all throughout this book because, like so many codependent relationships, the end was not a discrete event but more a series of letting go. Initially, it ended over the phone. Kyle was fed up about us not spending enough time together. I remembered sitting on the couch in the living room of my apartment. It was nighttime and I had not bothered to close the blinds of the giant bay window. I sat barefoot, surrounded by papers and books from the studying I had been doing before he called, and I listened to him tell me we were through, or he could not do it anymore—I do not remember which it was.

The week following was brutal. I felt numb and confused, relieved yet heartbroken. At the end of the week, Kyle showed up on my doorstep, looking so tall and handsome yet distant and sad, to transactionally exchange belongings with me. We did that. But that was also the time when we talked about why things were not working and he asked me to go to the courthouse with him to get married. When I shook my head no, his final question to me was why I could not marry him. When I told him, he became quiet and said, "I need to go," but by the end of the day, he had texted me to see if I wanted to go to church with him the following morning.

I remembered our talk at the end of that week. He called me, and we talked for hours about the mistakes we had made and about spirituality. I remembered the text he sent me after he finally had to hang up, "I hope we can work things out, Miss Azarcon, because you are too valuable to lose." I remembered, during that call, glancing down at the dating app I had downloaded, when he first broke up with me over the phone. I never even made a log in for it. It was useless to me now. Even so, I felt a little too afraid of our relational instability and uncertainty to delete it. I remembered most the way he looked at me when he saw that app, a week later. I remembered how I lost his heart forever in that moment. I desperately attempted to convince him that we should keep trying, but he was spiraling in fear and I was feeling strangled by his spiral. In the weeks following, things grew progressively worse. The attacks and mean comments intensified until I finally felt a resolve. I did not think God would want me to be here anymore. This was the end and though I was not really ready to release until then, I could physically no longer hold on. I knew deep down I could not stay any longer. I think he felt the same way.

The last time we talked about our relationship was over the phone. I was visiting home and sat in my parent's study surrounded by endless shelves of books. I listened and for once, we each spoke calmly and honestly about what we needed from the relationship. At the end of our conversation, we said peaceful goodbyes, wishing each other nothing but the best. It felt like standing in a clear and open space after a twister had ripped its way through. It felt like what I am feeling now, in this moment, as I write: in the wake of letting go, there is a gentleness. A softness toward all that has happened, and toward the future.

With grief, it seems that remembering turns into forgetting, and you come to remember nothing at all. That is mostly where I live now. It has been so long since I felt a tangible tenderness soft over my skin and heart that I have mostly forgotten what it is like. I have forgotten most of my relationship with Kyle. I have forgotten most of the things he said that made me love him and I have forgotten most of the things he said that made me want to stop loving him. I have forgotten when we were together, when we were apart, and why. Sometimes however, tender memories pierce through the haze of remembering and forgetting, shattering me anew. They jolt me back into a lost life, animating feelings I thought were dead. In those moments, I learn over how to feel, how to lead with my heart and not with my head—like kissing with my eyes closed.

Tenderness reminds me of something I have come to believe as true: I do not think we ever really recover from loving someone. While love for the individual can fade, the effects of having loved are irreversible. I am sometimes still amazed at how exquisite loving Kyle was. I shed so much ink and tears over him that it came to feel like blood; like the very life and essence that ran through my veins. My love for Kyle flowed through me like a river creating a canyon. First, it softened me. Next, it expanded me. Then, it split me open, gaping wide. The thing about such a phenomenon is that the rock that gave birth to a canyon is never the same. Never again will that spot be forgotten or filled with solid sediment. Yet, canyons are not empty—they are simply transformed. A new landscape is created. Rivers keep flowing and the canyon becomes a place of peace and beauty, rather than a place of devastation. It becomes something big and mysterious that tells a story. That is what tenderness has become to me and this is the letter that helped me realize how I did not want tenderness to die. I wanted to keep it alive.

August 2018

TENDERNESS

Tonight, out of nowhere, I remembered Kyle kissing me one Saturday morning. I remembered specifically how he paused in the middle to whisper, "I love you." It is funny how a memory so useless can wash over you in a new way. What struck me this time was the recollection of Kyle pausing to bare his heart to me—a rare memory of sweetness piercing through the haze of anger and indifference that has colored my memories of late.

I remember another kiss. Kyle was holding my head in his hands and he told me that I was the only girl that he had kissed for more than just the sake of kissing. Then he brushed my hair behind my ear, leaned in, and kissed me again. To share this sacred intimacy of the heart that he had not shared with anyone else, cultivated a sense of bonding—a sense of knowing and holding his heart, a feeling that I craved in a relationship with him. It made me feel like I was the only girl that he loved and would ever love. Even though he dated other girls during periods when we were broken up, I always felt like *we* were different—like, "I love you" was different when he said it to me. Once, he told me that every day of our breakup that he was not with me, that he was with another woman, he longed for me: physically, relationally, spiritually, and intellectually.

I longed for him too. Even when we were together, I longed for heart intimacy with Kyle. I sometimes felt that his heart was in a lockbox. I simultaneously felt like I was the code to the lockbox and like I could never quite open it. I remember a love that was intoxicating and just beyond my reach. Yet, in this memory of the whispered, "I love you," I saw Kyle in a different light. In this memory, I saw a split second when maybe the lockbox had sprung open and I saw the real Kyle baring the affection behind any affectations.

THE STRENGTH OF TENDERNESS

In the wake of that memory, I felt something I have not had the bravery to acknowledge until now—remorse. My regret over how I handled the end of our relationship feels shrouded in shame, like a dark secret. It feels like I would not survive the implications of it being brought to light. The truth is, I have been running from the suggestion that the end was my fault. I have been carrying the accusation that I hurt him beyond repair, an idea too hideous to be acknowledged until now, because it means his absence in my life is something I created.

Now, I have begun to accept his absence, in all its dimensions. I have felt all the ways he loved me and all the ways he hurt me gently washing out of my emotions, like suds from my hair under the warmth of shower water—an intermingling of the fresh and new with the dirty and stale. One bleeds in as the other bleeds out, leaving behind something soft and bare.

In this moment of tenderness, my heart is both of these things—soft and bare. I have a heart that has learned to beat without Kyle's love while brave enough to face the unattractive truths that lie within. Perhaps this is the final great grief of releasing Kyle: a deep sorrow that I wounded someone who I only ever wanted to give my softest self to. But with love, we do not merely give our softest selves. With the deepest love, we give all of ourselves. Yes, our best and our brightest but also our deepest and darkest— our wounds along with our triumphs of character.

The unattractive truth that lies within is that we were *both* loving in broken ways. I loved Kyle with fear as much as I did fervor. My deep need for him to make me okay prevented me from being honest. It caused me to withhold the full force of who I was and what I wanted in our relationship, wordlessly asking him to do the same. In fear of living without him, I tried to shape and force him into becoming who I needed him to be, instead of the person he was telling me all along (through his doubts, actions, and often over-bearing demands) he wanted to become. I placed on him the burden of my insecurities, asked him to heal me, and called it love.

Before I was able to face a world where Kyle did not love me, I could not acknowledge my part in the dismantling of our relationship. I extended myself much understanding for my actions and I wished that Kyle would have done the same. I saw the way I fumbled through our messy ending as fatal to our love. I saw the unraveling of our relationship as the final thing I could have done differently to change the outcome of his love for me. In this most recent memory of the softness we shared, I felt a deep desire to go back and change things—to carry Kyle's heart and vulnerability with more delicacy, because those were the things I wanted the most.

There was a tenderness I wanted to experience with Kyle and a tenderness I wanted to give Kyle. I never quite figured out how to give myself gently to him in the way I wanted to. I could never quite find a way to tell him how much I loved him and how I wanted to be with him, no matter what we had to work through. The first three times he told me he loved me, I said "thank you," even though I had known for a long time before then that I loved him and wanted to marry him. It was like kissing with my eyes open. I wanted heart intimacy, but I was afraid—afraid of things not working out, afraid of his disapproval, afraid if I said or did the wrong thing he would recoil even more. Maybe this is why the memory of tenderness is full of such wistful sadness. It is the echo of the "what if" I have been silencing. It turns up the volume of the thought that if I had been able to be as tender toward him as I wanted to be, he would have found a way to give that back to me.

I think again of what his face looked like when he saw the dating app on my phone—the moment I lost his tenderness toward me. I think if I could have found the words to express to him what my heart was feeling at that moment, I might have said something like this—"I don't want anyone on that app. I just want you. I have always only ever wanted you. But I'm afraid. Will you love me anyway? I want you to love me as much as I love you. Will you love me like that?" Of course, I did not find those words. It is rare in life that we do. Most of us will never have that movie moment where we finally find the words to unleash our most vulnerable truths in a way that cataclysmically shifts the whole story. The truth is, I did not need those words. I had been telling Kyle I was afraid all along. In real life, we speak with our actions, our wounds, and in the broken ways we love. Speaking with our words comes later, when we sit down to do the hard work of learning to love healthfully and honestly. As much as Kyle had all along been telling me he could not love me in the way I needed him to, I was wordlessly asking him to love me beyond my fears. His inability to do that in the moment was his "no." Without ever asking the question or hearing the word, I received the only answer I needed.

At times, I have been unable to see the broken ways I loved Kyle and all the ways they shaped our toxic dynamic. At other times, all I have seen are the deficiencies of my love for Kyle. In different seasons I have given both too much credit for the way our story ended. Both are about perfection, or lack thereof—I used to think becoming perfect would have secured Kyle's love for me. I told myself that story for seven years and it never became true. Nothing ever made me the only girl he cared for or allowed us to last—nothing I did could force Kyle to choose to wholly love me or to let me into his heart. I remember in moments like that kiss, an experience of feeling wholly loved. Now I can see that while those moments were real, they were incomplete. I never really held his whole heart to begin with and you cannot lose something you never truly had.

Perhaps what I feel washing over me in the residues of tenderness, is truth. The truth is that love will never be perfect, even when I am able to love another person with the strength and patience I wish I would have had the fortitude to love Kyle

LOSING YOU, FINDING ME

with. If I could go back and change some of the ways I loved Kyle, I would. I hurt Kyle, regardless of how much I tried or desired not to. I am sorry and he may never know that. Here, I see a strength in tenderness: a softness to remember that which still stings and the softness to see my heart as it is, not as condemned nor self-righteous, but as authentically and imperfectly beating. In tenderness, I find the strength to acknowledge regret and remorse, and release it.

THE PAIN OF TENDERNESS

In the same deep chamber of my heart where tenderness resides, are more memories, like the time I washed Kyle's feet (to symbolize my forgiveness toward his past), while we listened to what I thought would be our wedding dance song. He read a letter that I had written for that exact moment, a long time before, when I only hoped that we would be back together one day. I remember him cuddling up next to me afterward and I asked him what he was thinking. He replied that he was trying to think of a way to propose, at that moment, without it being "lame." I remember him nestling his head next to mine and telling me he did not know if he deserved me. There are probably a million more memories like this, a mental viewfinder of all the tender times that we shared.

It is hard to remember these. It is hard to hold them next to the end of our relationship and realize that the same person I went so sweetly deep with was the same person who felt so cold and distant at the end. The reality of both is hard to understand, so I forget one to cope with the other. Tenderness is difficult to remember because it requires softness and strength at the same time, a recognition of love and a subsequent release. Remembering tenderness can feel like a vortex, sucking me back into the elusive happy moments of the past. At the same time, it can feel like a black hole, creating a gaping emptiness in the present. It is easier to let a tender heart die a gradual death to callousness and self-sufficiency, than to remember a deep sweetness in love that is now gone and recognize a deep desire for that kind of love, which is now unmet. Even so, I think that tenderness is worth fighting for. The truth is that my love for Kyle, broken as it was, had moments of purity too. Those moments changed me and opened me in many ways. To have gone so deep and have been so delicate with another person is an experience incomparable to any other. As much as I am forgetting this man, the way I loved and experienced love through knowing him is not something I want to forget.

Maybe the sentiment of tenderness reminds me of Kyle because he was tender. That was probably his best quality, the strongest bond that kept me tied to him for so long. No matter the magnitude of a blowup or disappointment, there were also moments and ways in which he cherished me with a tenderness that some women never experience in a relationship. It was his exquisite strength gleaming through all the muck and mire of our relational weaknesses. I was afraid that no one would ever be so gentle with me again, so I stayed. I tolerated the cutting remarks, the controlling behaviors, and all the toxic dynamics because I was afraid to lose his tenderness towards me.

All along, I thought this breakup meant tenderness could not exist in my life anymore. When Kyle and I first broke up, my one remaining hope for tenderness was in another relationship and I doubted whether I would ever find it there. This hope felt too risky so all I allowed myself to feel was the anger and bitterness from all the ways Kyle and I hurt each other. Yet, something is happening as I am able to remember the tenderness I shared with Kyle and let it go: recognizing it enables the final release of my love for him. It enables me to see the good things about Kyle that coexisted with the bad. It helps me to see the years I spent with him not as entirely wasted, but as time spent learning about love; making mistakes but being transformed by the pockets of beauty found between us.

THE GRACE OF TENDERNESS

This is the grace of tenderness, not as a sentiment toward Kyle, but as a softness towards all that happened—the love and hurt alike. In this space, I see a different side of Kyle, past the callousness and the person who hurt me. In the memory of that kiss, for a split second, I saw the Kyle who loved me the best he knew how.

In the light of tenderness, I can see the love and brokenness side by side. It would be easy to look back on this relationship and see Kyle as the villain and me as the heroine. But I do not think that reflects the truth of relationships in real life. Even when one person crosses the lines of trust and mistreats you, that does not make them all evil, nor you all good. We are all broken and fractured to different degrees, mixed bags of wonderful and difficult. There is something about tenderness washing over us that illuminates the beauty and the scars in a very soft way—loosening my grasp on the wrongs done to me. It allows me to acknowledge my own part, the way I plugged my deep need for healing into Kyle's dysfunction, making our mess worse. Welling up inside me is an acknowledgment that, for all the ways I differed from Kyle in our relationship, there was one way in which I was the same. I too made mistakes. I too was somewhere in the middle of irresistible and impossible. I too was in process. And I feel sorry. Not so much regret as an acknowledgment that, even though I tried so hard to do things perfectly, I was chasing impossible. I was believing the lie that I could heal another's dysfunctions with the force of my codependent love, thinking that if I saved him, his love would be enough to save me. For that, I am also sorry. I scratched down a few words in my journal the other day from this place of my mistakes, from tenderness. I wrote them to the Kyle who opened his heart to me.

Dear Kyle,

I gave you my best. I am sorry that, even so, I hurt you. I hope you find someone you love in ways love was not able to work with me. May she always treat your heart with care and tenderness.

With these words, I felt myself letting go of responsibility and judgment alike. I felt my heart untangling itself from the obligation to make better all the mistakes I made. I felt myself releasing Kyle from the debt of what I wanted him to be to me. In tenderness toward the past, I find a gentleness of heart toward the good pieces that irreversibly changed me, a remembrance with quiet thankfulness. In tenderness toward the future, I find a willingness to open my heart to love in all its jagged, messy glory again. I do not have to surrender all that was good in the past to all that was bad. Tenderness softens, which is the very thing that seems it might kill you to feel, but somehow makes it possible to keep on living after all that has happened. This is the grace of tenderness: forgiveness for Kyle, for me, and for all the ways the past fell short.

THE FORWARD MOTION OF TENDERNESS

In broken-heartedness, as with every other type of pain, our inclination is to value forgetfulness. We hold it as a marker of forward motion, a milestone of our progress. I think something sacred occurs when we find the strength to remember the good that happened alongside the pain. The movement of remembrance is not like the linear forwardness of forgetting, but rather a dynamic process of expansion. It enlarges our hearts, allowing little pieces of the love we lost to be found in other places, seeping in from other sources. As this process grows us outward, it also pulls us forward. By revealing to us love in other places, it allows us to release the love of the past, the love that is no longer serving us in the present. From this process of expansion and propulsion, we find in our hearts a sacred space, where our pasts are washed over by a new present, and we are shaped to receive our futures.

So with this recent memory of tenderness, I am reminded that as the flame I carried for Kyle extinguishes, I should strive to protect the little flicker of tenderness towards love in my heart. Tenderness keeps us soft and softness keeps us wild. Somehow, this memory that I have deeply loved is a promise for the future. I want to remember that tenderness exists and is not lost, but simply transforming. I want to remember that I have and am capable of loving beyond a sweetness I knew to be possible. Fighting for tenderness means fighting for the gentle trickle of all these things back into my heart and life.

A few nights ago, I was thinking of the realization that I am worthy of someone loving me as much as I love him. I told God that if the love that is coming next would not love me as much as I am willing to love him, I should just give up on the idea of another love entirely. I was nearly asleep but as soon as I thought this, a very strong thought popped into my head, *"Who told you that he will not love you as much as you love him?"* That was special. That assurance may take some time to come to fruition. Nevertheless, it is an assurance that here in the stillness, tenderness is growing.

DEATH

yle is mostly dead to me. Not in the way that you mean when you are angry at someone and forbid them ever into your life again. Rather, in the way that I do not know who he is anymore or who he has become. The bright-eyed man I talked with for hours in my living room, the night we first met, is long gone. He is like a memory from childhood that feels unreal, a shadow, a silhouette, but one you know existed because someone else remembers it too.

A few weeks ago, I came across some love notes from him. I didn't even know I still had them since I thought I threw them all out a long time ago. I had written these particular ones in a journal, from the morning after we got back together with the intention of getting married. When I read them, they did not move me. First, I shrugged because they were what they were—a memory that was happy in the past but irrelevant to the present. Then, I giggled a little. Reading the term "love of my life" used to describe me felt so foreign, like putting on a pair of running shoes you have not worn in a long time.

Sometimes when I am quite tired, I will forget

people's names, people I have known for a long time. A few months ago, this happened while I was talking about Kyle. I called him "what's his name, that guy I used to date." Then, I gasped internally, because in seven years, I had never for a moment forgotten his name. And I knew that the love was dying.

I think that really, the love started to die while we were together because different pieces of us, as individuals, were dying. We were both walking away from childhood paradigms, but in different directions. In this transformative process, little pieces of who we each used to be died. In these deaths, the death of my love for Kyle and the death of who I used to be, I was reborn. I was freed into something limitless and deep, something that felt a bit like taking deep gulps of fresh mountain air. Even so, the deaths were a release, a loss, which was slow and painful.

I started writing this letter as I drove into Glacier National Park, Montana. I remember looking out the window at the mountains and scratching down these thoughts, as they rolled into my head. The scene outside my window reminded me of mountains I had seen with Kyle, right before we decided to date the very first time. On our way to a camping trip, we had carved our way through one of the many forests in Northern California. It was just us, in his shaky old car, under a giant moon that ricocheted its light off the commanding, slate grey mountains. As much as these mountains marked a beginning for Kyle and I, there was something about the mountains in Montana that made me feel a finality to the end of us. Perhaps, it is because mountains seem unconquerable, but we are laid under a carved stone, a tiny piece of the mountain, when death finally conquers us. More so, it felt like majesty; like something wild, alive, and free had fought its way out of me and was now big and commanding, something that had gradually edged Kyle out of my heart. Whatever it was, I knew he was not with me there. I no longer carried him in my heart. There, under the stone and the sky, I made peace with what no longer was and what had not been for a long time. This is how I learned to accept death, to accept that I could not pull around the past forever, because the present had pulled me. For so long, I had felt like I was dying, slipping slowly into inescapable darkness and sleep. But that was only our love. Me, I was awakening, opening gradually to the light of morning and a new life. So, I wrote a eulogy to our love and what had been—a love letter that opened my heart to the present unfolding around me.

September 2018

DEATH

My mother said that she would like to take my littlest sister to the farmer's market this weekend. What a throwback. Many years ago, Kyle and I took her to the farmer's market. At this time, she was young and obsessed with a song called "Piggy Plum Pie." We taught Kyle this song and the three of us sang it together on the way back from the market. I shared this story with my mom because it reminds me of an era gone by. "Where did that man go?" she asked. "He was a different person then," she remarked. *We both were.* She mentioned a camping trip we took when he and I were just falling in love. "He was so tender and attentive to you on the trip," she reminisced. "I thought, wow, this boy really loves my daughter." We have a picture from that trip. It is a group photo, but he and I are leaning into each other, like two halves of a singular whole. He is wearing a shirt with gold lettering that reads in Italian, "a beautiful girl, I sometimes love." The story of our relationship.

I am camping again this weekend, for only the second time since I was on that trip. It seems that every time I go camping, something significant is about to unfold. This weekend I am sleeping under the stars, learning to be a little wilder. This weekend he is at an expensive, suburban soccer party with my cousin and is probably doing the same types of things he did at these parties that caused friction when we were together. It does not matter because my life is released from the measuring stick of his life—of comparing my progress, opinions, and emotions to his. Yet, the contrast reminds me of what different people we have become.

At first, that was the hardest part of this grief. It was not that we did not end up together. It was the feeling that the person I loved for so long no longer existed. The man I met, I could not find. I could not run home to his heart—that heart was no longer there. The heart I loved and fought for until the end. I watched it die a slow, painful death until all I held were ashes: the gritty ruin of something that used to be.

Over time this has become a sort of freedom to me, because what I was looking for in his heart was only ever halfway there. The other half was compensated for by hope and optimism for a reality that never came to be. Knowing that his heart is fully gone has released me to hope for a heart in which what I desire is fully there. It has also released me to inhabit the fullness of my own heart.

A few weeks ago, I walked to my car in the crisp morning air, enjoying the warm sun. I felt light and happy with joy bubbling up inside. I realized that what I was feeling was freedom—a freedom to fully be and love myself. I have been growing in hearing God. The night before, I had laid my hands on a girl I had never met before and perceived that she had two sisters and she was the middle. The week before, I had prayed for a friend's wife with my church group. She was not there but her husband told us she was suffering from headaches. As we prayed, I sensed that she had also been struggling with fatigue for about one year. I asked if this was true and her husband said "Yes, exactly one year." After we prayed for her, she stopped having headaches altogether. These things make me feel like I am becoming a better version of myself, the self I was always meant to be. Yet, I do not think I would have discovered these pieces of myself if I had stayed with Kyle. My heart was too invested in becoming who I thought he wanted me to be, instead of discovering the parts of me that are most beautiful, powerful, and life-giving. As I pondered this, I felt a lightness because I was free from the hold of any voices in my life telling me who I should or should not be. I see now with Kyle, that we both loved with half of our hearts. For half my heart he called out life and so, I gave him the other half. The half I let him control and let his love define. That half has only come alive now that he is gone. Somehow, in losing all of his heart, I am gaining all of mine.

I didn't write these stories with the intent to expose flaws. In every relationship, there are imperfections. In every relationship that ends, there is hurt and anger no matter how agreeable the ending is. My imperfections impacted Kyle and his imperfections impacted me. These stories are not about those imperfections or what happened between us. They are not about what went wrong or where the responsibility is distributed. They are about the fact that a beautiful but complicated man walked into my life and deeply impacted so much of my story. Somewhere along the line, our story ended but mine continued. And I have to keep telling my story.

There is a beach we used to go to together. We would drive down the PCH, my hair whipping in the wind. We would sneak into this hidden cove to sit on the natural stone stairs. I remember this beach because we prayed there, asking God to allow us to get married. Kyle wrapped his arms around me and we looked at the sea, praying that we knew there were differences that frustrated us, but we wanted to spend our lives together—would God help us? I used to go to that beach when we were broken up over the years, before our final break up. I would sit on the stairs alone and reflect. I loved how watching the waves reminded me of waiting on a promise and the faithfulness of God. Once, after driving past the beach, I wrote to God.

Dear God,

I like to go to the cove because it reminds me of your faithfulness. It reminds me of the truth that you know and hold the corner of my heart where longing dwells. You heard my prayer and you have not forgotten. I like to sit there and watch the water, remembering my prayer request is like the waves of the sea. The day we prayed, it washed very powerfully on the shores of my heart and now it has gone out—one little request being tossed about in the mighty, uncontrollable, good, vastness of you. In this space, it is being refined. Like the waves, it will return. It will again kiss the Earth and move sand on the shore. But how it returns, what it bears, and what it has been refined into, remains unknown.

The last time I went to that beach was before Kyle and I got back together for the last time. I went alone, to sing over this sacred place the songs God had placed on my heart for Kyle and me. I stepped out of my car and descended the long wooden steps leading to the cove. I had to stop at the bottom of the steps because it was raining that day, and the wind and rain were too powerful for me to go any further. The storm grew and I soon had to return to my car. Yet, I stayed at the beach. I sat in my car and sang the songs I had come to sing. One of them was a song I had been singing over Kyle for months. It was about the love of God flooding our lives like a storm at sea. It compared this love to torrential rain, love so consuming it buried past mistakes at the bottom of a storm-tossed sea.

When I left the beach that day, the storm was so heavy I had to change radio stations. I browsed and landed on a song I had never heard before called Send the Rain. There was a preacher who released blessings as the gospel choir sang. Driving away from the beach where Kyle and I had first prayed to get married, I heard him speak that the rain foreshadowed harvest. It promised that every prayer uttered in a dry season was like a seed about to break forth.

I have not gone back to that beach since. It feels like it is a sacred relic of another era, an era I want to leave as is. But the beach is still there, and the waves still come ashore, reminding me of a poem I wrote the one other time I camped since knowing Kyle.

But dare not go where they've been before
Glistening wet dried up as land
Where once we walked hand in hand
And all that's left are faint white marks upon the sand

WILD

I have a five-year journal. It asks a question a day for five years. I am currently completing my second one. I bought my first one after Kyle and I broke up the very first time. It was uncharacteristic of me being as frugal as I am, but his birthday had passed the day before, so being heartsick and lovesick, I bought one. The question, in this journal, for February 15, is "write down the cure for a broken heart." This year, I wrote "Leaning into grief. Hope for a better tomorrow that leads to the cultivation of a new life." If you did not read a single one of my letters, you could probably read that sentence and navigate pretty well.

This short, deep statement reminds me a lot of navigating grief with God. You want Him to write you a letter, a manual on how to get out of bed and what clothes to wear, what to eat, and every detail in between when your heart aches so much. It seems that He instead whispers quietly, one deep word at a time. As you string those words together over time, they become a complete sentence, a complete story- one that is beautiful, sweet, and full of meaning.

Throughout grief, I have come to realize that God has

written a letter in Jesus, and that letter is love. Regardless of your thoughts on Jesus, He was the man of radical love. His life was love, His death was love, His return from the grave was love. Over and over again, when I am lost I go back to that—Jesus, love. In the end, I did not really need a manifesto on grief. All I needed was to realign with love over and over again. The letters merely helped because they guided me to that. In the end, the road was always going to love.

Love will always be my adventure. The thing about love is that it is dangerous. It entails risk and heartache, wandering and finding your way again, losing and finding anew, breaking and being made whole. Love is not tame—but love makes you brave. It teaches you to fall back in love with life, with the wild spirit inside of yourself, with the big deep breaths that fill your lungs, and with the God that inhabits them all. It teaches you how to be alive again. It resurrects you from the grave of grief. I guess in a way, the cure to a broken heart is also falling in love. But, not in the way I thought I would fall in love again.

To me, no place more perfectly captures falling in love in a way that is wild and free, and measureless and brave, than Montana. In January, I suggested to my sister that, for her birthday gift, we plan a girl's trip. She loves to travel, and I thought we might visit Boston or New York or Paris. She told me that she would like to go somewhere outside. In high school, a few of our friends had visited Montana and I remembered being surprised by its beauty in pictures. "How about Montana?" I suggested. I googled a few pictures of the state and clicked my favorite one. It happened to be a picture of Glacier National Park and it was decided that is where we would go: Big Sky Country. The sky in Montana lives up to its name. It is so big. It envelops you, filling you with a sense of quiet, and at the same time, measureless possibility. Here, in this place of lakes, glaciers, moose, and bears- the completed work my heart had been moving toward was reflected back to me.

One of the most meaningful gifts Kyle ever gave to me was a yellow rose bush for my birthday. With it, he gave me a card that read "I am a rose of Sharon, a lily of the valleys."[1] He explained that this was an expression of being, like a wildflower, beautiful and delicate but also exposed and in need of protection. He kept the plant with the intention of caring and tending it, as he wanted to care for and tend my heart. The rose bush ultimately died because Kyle forgot to water it. For a long time, I felt like that flower—a heart that Kyle gave up on watering, withering away from the lack of his love. In Montana, I felt again like a rose of Sharon, a flower of the valleys. I felt simultaneously wild and delicate. Yet, I was not so much in need of protection, as I had been with Kyle because I had love. Love is strange in the way that it is risky, unpredictable, and unknown. It is dangerous but it somehow protects at the same time. Every time you fall, it catches you. It grows you a little deeper, a little more beautiful, like a flower. As I sat by the Montana campfire,

---

1   Song of Solomon 2:1New International Version

I opened a brand-new journal and began writing this letter.

September 2018

WILD

"Let a new life happen to you."[2] This is a quote that has been on my heart for a long time. Over the past year, it has slowly played out, but it has never felt as complete as it does now. Now, I am in Montana, a reminder that sometimes, life looks different than we would expect. My original idea of a vacation was a European trip with sexy outfits and bougie food. Instead, I found myself camping in East Glacier Montana, sleeping on the ground and wearing polar fleece.

On my first night in Montana, my chronic cough disappeared. I woke the next morning, after sleeping nearly thirteen hours. Even though I had been freezing all night, I woke feeling more refreshed and pain-free than I had in a long time. Over my time here, I have climbed a glacier, been chased off the beach by a baby moose, and belly laughed in kayaks with new trail friends.

I think we forget that the human body needs wide open spaces—to breathe, to be unhurried, to learn to be natural again. I think the human heart also needs open, empty, barren seasons where neither the end nor the beginning is in sight. Sometimes, this entails

2   Waheed, Nayyirah. Untitled. https://www.nayyirahwaheed.com

not knowing when the climb will end, if you are strong enough to make it, if you will have enough food for the journey. I wonder if a wilderness season is something like that.

Maybe a wilderness season is not so much wilderness as it is wild. Maybe the silence, the space, the unknowing, the climbing, the places far from comfort or others, are an invitation for us to learn to rediscover ourselves—to pause, to breathe, to learn to be natural again, a space to let your heart expand, to whisper what it is feeling, what it is becoming and what it wants to be. The beauty of this is that in the wild, we find wonder.

There was something about Montana that restored my childlike sense of wonder. For the first time in a long time, I felt the freedom to pause and feel human again. There was something about the way that nature filled me. It made crisp air crisper and the green greener, filling my lungs with life, air, and laughter that I had not felt for a long time.

Even though this place was physically challenging, there was an un-hurriedness to it that brought me alive. Everywhere you looked there were wide mountains and fields of flowers inviting you to pause on the ascent and take pictures of all the beautiful treasures along the way. I wonder if this collection of letters was unknowingly like that—me taking pictures of all the beautiful things along the way, in my journey to becoming wild.

One of the high points of this trip for me, both

literally and emotionally, was hiking Grinnell Glacier. This was something I had wanted to do since we decided to visit Montana, but we missed the boat ride that would cut four miles off of our hike and I did not think I would make it. This little old lady named Pat looked at me and said, "You can make it. I know you can." She was right. As I climbed, I realized something. All along, I thought Montana would be about proving myself, about proving I was strong enough, and proving I could conquer the wilderness. But Montana was not about proving myself. It was about uncovering myself. The fortitude to make it to the top of Grinnell Glacier had been in me all along. I just had to give it the chance to show itself. It is similar to my wilderness season. I do not need to prove that I am strong. All along, strength has been developing in me and pushing me to new heights. All through the wilderness, I have been becoming wild.

In many ways, I feel this marks the close of a season. The wilderness has made me wild and the wild pulls me into wonder. It is an unhurried surrender, rather than a driving push. I think that wonder looks a little bit like this:

At some point, you have to stop being afraid. You have to stop worrying about who is in your life and who is not, what will happen and what will not, what has happened happening again. You have to stop worrying about who will love you and who will not. At some point, you have to go out and live your life because it is waiting for you. It is waiting to be discovered in places you would never think to look, on the ground, under the stars, and in wide, empty spaces. It is waiting for you to take its picture. It is waiting for you to belly laugh, to run through fields of flowers, to marvel at moose, and to walk to nowhere in particular. Most of all, it is waiting for you to discover that there is no greater wild than finding your heart inside of His.

Last night, I stepped off the plane, went home, and showered. I traded bandannas and vests for mascara and softly curled hair because I had to return to civilization. Despite that, I realized the most amazing thing. The wild is not in Montana. The wild is here, today. It is waking up every morning to the new surprises God's heart and God's grace unfold. When you discover your heart inside of His, the wild is not a place or a new adventure. The wild is inside you. The wild is you running and dancing freely to the music that the God living inside you has always been playing.

ABOUT THE AUTHOR

Chelsea Azarcon knew she wanted to be an author since she was a child. Inspired by her own challenges with health, she decided to become a doctor instead. She now practices naturopathic medicine in Northern California and is passionate about helping people find healing from the inside out. In her spare time you can find her training her service dog, Rey, baking with a healthy twist, and exploring the outdoors. She loves the beach, fresh cut flowers, and dancing with little skill but plenty of enthusiasm. To learn more about Dr. Chelsea, you can visit her website chelseaazarcon.com or follow her on Instagram under the handle @naturallydrchelsea.

CPSIA information can be obtained
at www.ICGtesting.com
Printed in the USA
BVHW052217301222
655376BV00014B/451